TEENS ~
POSITIVE THOUGHTS ✛
AFFIRMATIONS ⚌
POSITIVE ACTIONS ▶

Facilitator Reproducible Activities for Groups and Individuals

Ester R.A. Leutenberg

Carol Butler, MS Ed, RN, C

Illustrated by
Amy L. Brodsky, LISW-S

wholeperson
Health & Wellness Publishers
Duluth, Minnesota

wholeperson
Health & Wellness Publishers

101 West 2nd Street, Suite 203
Duluth, MN 55802

800-247-6789

books@WholePerson.com
WholePerson.com

Teens ~ Positive Thoughts + Affirmations = Positive Actions
Facilitator Reproducible Activities for Groups and Individuals

Printed in the United States of America

10 9 8 7 6 5 4 3 2 1

Editorial Director: Carlene Sippola
Art Director: Mathew Pawlak

Library of Congress Control Number: 2015917442
ISBN: 978-157025-340-9

Teens ~ Positive Thoughts + Affirmations = Positive Actions

Purpose of the Workbook

To offer teens interesting and insightful sessions focusing on ways positive thoughts and affirmations lead to positive actions.

To provide teens with Take-Away Skills to apply to real life events and situations.

To present examples of positive life skills to teens ...

Set positive, attainable goals.

Define steps to reach each goal.

Consider possible outcomes.

Relate skills learned in sessions to real-life.

To set measureable goals for educational and treatment planning.

To define ways that skills gained in sessions are used in life.

Teens will be encouraged to focus on positive thoughts, affirmations, and actions:

Acknowledge that thoughts and words determine views of self, others, and the world.

Monitor and reframe thoughts.

Compose positive affirmations, always with accompanying actions.

See their words and graphics daily on their *My Affirmations and More* displays.

Identify and exemplify positive traits/qualities in self and others.

Become aware that they grow from their worst and best experiences.

Prove "It can be done."

Use social media for positive purposes.

Cultivate enthusiasm for personal passions and for issues beyond self.

Recharge emotionally, intellectually, physically, spiritually, and socially.

Exercise emotional self-protection, empowerment, and creative resilience.

Experience the helper's high.

View the past through the lens of learning.

Turn obstacles into opportunities.

Forge their futures with hope, vision, and action.

**To provide opportunities for teens to demonstrate
that workable affirmations are not just notions.
Affirmations are ideas:**
From the brain that believes,
To the hand that writes,
To the mouth that speaks,
To the person who puts them into action.

Teens will mold themselves into "Yay-Sayers" who say ...

"Yay" to whatever happens: "I'll be strengthened by it."

"Yay" to today's challenges: "I'll do my best."

"Yay" to compassion: "I'll help."

"Yay" to the future: "Today's actions make my tomorrows."

Format of the Workbook

Introduction for Teen Participants

Distribute the *Introduction for Teen Participants*, page vii, as an overview before the first activity. This page helps motivate teens for upcoming sessions.

Cover Page for Each Chapter

The cover page helps the facilitator to stimulate discussion about the quotation and to select topics.

Distribute each chapter's cover page before the chapter's sessions.

This preview provides an inspirational quotation and descriptions of each handout to spark interest.

Teens may refer to the cover page list of each handout, and vote on which activity to do next.

Take-Away Skills for each Chapter Following each Chapter Cover Page

Conditions and Behavior, Frequency and Duration, and/or *Accomplishment* statements for each activity may be used in educational and/or treatment planning. They may also be used to measure progress toward goals. These skills promote real life outcomes and behavioral changes. *See page v, Take-Away Skills.*

Educational and Treatment Session Skills are listed on the facilitator page on the reverse side of each handout. Teens will use oral, written and creative expression skills, give and receive peer feedback, and demonstrate skills specific to each handout.

Chapters

1. **Affirmations**
2. **Traits/Qualities**
3. **Challenges**
4. **Thought Re-programming**
5. **Enthusiasm**
6. **Self-Determination**
7. **Positive Actions**
8. **Recap**

Versatility

An individual chapter may serve as a workshop.

Sessions may be strategically selected to match the skills that would benefit specific teens.

Most handouts are applicable to individual or group use.

Creative expression, games, skits, and other skill-building experiences are provided.

Reproducible Handouts

Facilitators may photocopy and distribute the handouts as they appear in this book, or they may personalize them with white out and/or add text as desired and then use as a master to photocopy.

Information on the Reverse Side of Each Handout for the Facilitator

I. **Purpose** - The goals for the teens in each session.

II. **Skills** - Behavioral objectives and competencies for the session.

III. **Possible Activities** - Ways to present topics and responses to elicit.

IV. **Enrichment Activities** - Additional learning experiences, ways to conclude or follow up.

Take-Away Skills

Take-Away Skills …

- follow each chapter cover page for each of the reproducible activity handouts in each chapter.
- describe the behaviors that teens are expected to demonstrate when they are away from the session.
- demonstrate that new competencies have been applied to real life situations.
- show results.
    example: a teen writes a journal entry each night describing what went well.
- allow self-reporting.
    example: a teen reports that stress level decreased from #5 to #2 after thought substitution.
- are easily countable.
    example: a teen states aloud or says to self, a positive affirmation during times of stress in 5 out of 5 opportunities.
- answer these questions:
    Did the desired behavior occur?
    What is the evidence?
    To what extent?

Conditions and Behavior (1), *Frequency and Duration* (2), and/or *Accomplishment* (3) **statements**
    for each activity may be used in educational and/or treatment planning, and also used to measure progress toward goals. These skills promote real life outcomes and behavioral changes.

Three Types of Take-Away Skills

Conditions and Behavior – a skill or healthy habit to replace a previous less effective behavior or habit.
    Now I … *(less effective or undesired behavior)*
    When I … *(when do I do this?)*
    Instead I will … *(more effective or desired new behavior)* in __ out of __ opportunities.

Frequency and Duration – a skill or healthy habit not necessarily tied to a condition or previous behavior.
    I will *(describe the behavior)* _____ times per _____.

Accomplishment – an outcome that is a one-time accomplishment.
    I will *(describe the accomplishment)* by _____ (date).

Teens, and teen facilitators using this workbook, strive for skills that are developed during sessions to transfer into real life skills.

Monthly, photocopy the Teen Opportunity Journal, page viii, for each participant.

How to Present the Activity Handouts

> *"An affirmation a day keeps our negative thought away? Affirmations are like mental vitamins – words with power. They provide the exquisite supplementary positive thoughts to enhance and balance the barrage of negative events and thoughts we experience daily. Affirmations affirm our soul and empower our mind in a most positive and tangible way."*
>
> ~ Angie Karan Krezos

Chronology of Activities

Begin with Chapter 1, *Affirmations*.
   Teens transform thoughts into affirmations with accompanying actions.
   Teens begin their *My Affirmations and More* displays, and add items after each session.

When presenting Chapter 2, *Traits/Qualities*, introduce it with the handout A - Z Positive Traits, page 29.
   The list on this page is a resource for other activities in the chapter.
   All of the other handouts in this chapter may be presented in any order.

The Affirmations and More Display

Teens will post their positive thoughts and graphics on their own *My Affirmations and More* display.
In a location of their choice they will have a constant reminder of their discoveries from
   this workbook.

Creativity

Encourage teens to use positive visualization, graphic representation, and creative expression.
Assure participants that putting thoughts and feelings onto the paper is most important.
Explain that lyrics or poems need not rhyme.
Stress that theatrical training is not needed to write and/or act in skits.

Actions

Affirmations are accompanied by actions.
Activity handouts in sessions incorporate individual and team action.
Actions outside sessions apply skills to real life.
Games elicit personal applications of concepts, not "right" or "wrong" answers.

Growth

Teens will expand their imaginations to believe in themselves so that they can achieve their goals.
Teens will go beyond their comfort zones.
Teens will want to use their hands to help others.
Teens will learn to allow their hearts to care.

Opportunities

Teens will be encouraged to complete a *Teen Opportunity Journal* as homework. See page viii.

Introduction for Teen Participants

Whether we realize it or not, we talk to ourselves, all the time, every day.
Our self-talk affects how we see ourselves, others, and the world.
Self-talk affects our emotions and actions.

It sometimes seems that thoughts just pop into our heads.
They might!

But we decide…
Which thoughts we rent head space to.
Which thoughts we evict.

It may sound simple…
But, we can change our thoughts and change our lives.

Yet, it isn't always easy because …
We might believe put-downs from others.
We might have put ourselves down for so long that it has become a habit.
We might be unaware of the messages that bombard us.
We might not monitor our thoughts and therefore they run wild.

You can put into practice an equation.
Positive Thoughts + Affirmations = Positive Actions

The activities in this workbook will help you …
Decide what you want to believe about yourself.
Picture your beliefs.
Develop positive traits.
Navigate obstacles.
Re-program your negative thoughts.
Live life enthusiastically.
Determine your future.
Take possible actions.

Make your self-talk believable, positive, and powerful.
And then … make it real!

Teen Opportunity Journal

Name _____   Month _____

My Goal _____

Each day you will have an opportunity to reach your goal. Fill in the dates of the month in the top left box and check whether you had an opportunity to reach your goal WITHOUT Success (O) or whether you took the opportunity to reach your goal WITH Success (S).

MONTHLY CALENDAR

SUNDAY	MONDAY	TUESDAY	WEDNESDAY	THURSDAY	FRIDAY	SATURDAY
O☐ or S☐	O☐ or S☐	O☐ or S☐	O☐ or S☐	O☐ or S☐	O☐ or S☐	O☐ or S☐
O☐ or S☐	O☐ or S☐	O☐ or S☐	O☐ or S☐	O☐ or S☐	O☐ or S☐	O☐ or S☐
O☐ or S☐	O☐ or S☐	O☐ or S☐	O☐ or S☐	O☐ or S☐	O☐ or S☐	O☐ or S☐
O☐ or S☐	O☐ or S☐	O☐ or S☐	O☐ or S☐	O☐ or S☐	O☐ or S☐	O☐ or S☐
O☐ or S☐	O☐ or S☐	O☐ or S☐	O☐ or S☐	O☐ or S☐	O☐ or S☐	O☐ or S☐

Date	Notes

Teens ~ Positive Thoughts + Affirmations = Positive Actions

TABLE OF CONTENTS

(Continued on the next page)

Teens ~ Positive Thoughts + Affirmations = Positive Actions

TABLE OF CONTENTS *(continued)*

(Continued on the next page)

Teens ~ Positive Thoughts + Affirmations = Positive Actions

TABLE OF CONTENTS *(continued)*

Our Deepest Gratitude to
the following professionals who make us look good!

Editorial Director	–	Carlene Sippola
Cover Design	–	Joy Dey
Art Director	–	Mathew Pawlak
Editor and Lifelong Teacher	–	Eileen Regen, M.Ed., CJE
Proofreader Extraordinaire	–	Jay Leutenberg, CASA
Reviewer & Teen Teacher	–	Niki Tilicki, M.A.Ed.
Reviewer & Teen Counselor	–	Eileen Jonaitis, M.A.Ed.

AFFIRMATIONS ①

Do. Or do not. There is no try.

~ Yoda

Take-Away Skills

Conditions and Behavior (1), *Frequency and Duration* (2), and/or *Accomplishment* (3) statements for each activity may be used in educational and/or treatment planning, and also used to measure progress toward goals. These Take-Away skills promote real life outcomes and behavioral changes.

EXAMPLES

1. *Conditions and Behavior* – **a skill or healthy habit to replace a previous less effective behavior or habit.**
   - Now, I … *(less effective or undesired behavior).*
   - When I … *(when do I do this?),*
     instead I will … *(more effective or desired new behavior)* in _____ out of _____ opportunities.
2. **Frequency and Duration – a skill or healthy habit not necessarily tied to a condition or previous behavior.**
   - I will *(describe the behavior)* _____ times per _____.
3. **Accomplishment – an outcome that is a one-time accomplishment.**
   - I will *(describe the accomplishment)* by _____ *(date).*

CHAPTER 1 - Affirmations
Take-Away Skills Examples

Affirmations at Work

You can reprogram your negative *thoughts* with positive *affirmations*.
You will soon believe your positive thoughts which will lead to positive *actions*!

Affirmations are not just words!
Affirmations are not magic that alone will make things happen!

Affirmations are statements you tell yourself. Affirmations can become realities.

Imagine you are about to give a speech.
Place a check mark in front of the affirmation or thought that gives you the best chance of success:

_____ "I'll be tongue-tied." *(a negative affirmation coming from a negative thought).*
_____ "I am well prepared." *(a positive affirmation coming from a positive thought,).*

Affirmations are statements going beyond the reality of the
present into the creation of the future
through the words you use in the now.

~ Louise L. Hay

Effective affirmations are …

Positive to create the reality you want.
Personal and in your own words, the way you really talk.
Powerful to motivate your thoughts and actions.
In the present tense as if you already are who you want to be, or already have what you want.
Believable because you say you're "willing to …" or "working toward …" if necessary.
Achievable because you are taking action.
Short and sweet, easy to remember and repeat.

Affirmations program your conscious and subconscious mind to help you …

Reach goals.
Develop a positive self-image.
Change harmful behavior.
Reverse negative messages or put-downs from self and/or others.
Let go of resentment, fear, jealousy, etc.
Incorporate values, beliefs, acceptance, assertiveness, etc. into your identity.

Think about what you want. Believe it is a reality. Create your affirmation.

AFFIRMATIONS

Example:	My Own Affirmation …	My Action …
I believe in the power of affirmations		

Affirmations at Work: What Is More?

Affirmations combined with actions, repetition, and visualization work best.

Consider the example about giving a speech.
"I am well prepared" is believable when you actually did prepare.
"I have my Power Point presentation ready," is an action that proves you are prepared.

Actions

Create affirmations with their accompanying actions.

My Own Affirmation	My Actions
Ex: I have a healthy body build.	*Ex: I eat fresh fruits, veggies and lean protein.* *I walk a mile daily.* *I am free from toxic substances.*

Repetition

Put your affirmations where you'll see them
(wallet, mirror, computer, *My Affirmations and More* display, etc.).
Read them aloud when you wake up, before sleep, and several times during the day.
You may also talk to yourself in the mirror, or take a video on your phone
to play back for yourself, not others.
You will believe your affirmations when you hear your voice say them.

Visualization

Seeing is believing!
Imagine you want to own a car.
Picture the make, model, and color in your mind. Look at a photo of the car you want.
See yourself doing what's needed (passing your driving test, working to pay for it).
Take a selfie with your paycheck, or in front of the bank
where you have set up a special savings account for the purchase of your car.

Affirmations at Work: Put It All Together

Your display can be anything and anywhere:

Use a roll of large paper, poster board or cork board on wall space, notebook, scrapbook, sketchbook, or journal, web page, blog, or personal and private computer document.

POSSIBILITIES

Take pictures of your display for your phone or wallet.
Place positive quotations and affirmations around the borders.
Place a photo of yourself in the center, surrounded by positive images.
Use computer pictures, magazine clippings, sketches, words, slogans, lyrics, etc.
Glue items randomly in a collage, or create sections, or use the four corners for specifics.

POSSIBLE SECTIONS	POSSIBLE CORNERS
Career or job	Positive beliefs
Family	Positive goals
Friends	Positive media messages
Further education	Positive music and movies
Interests/hobbies	Positive people
Role models	Positive places
Who I want to become	Positive objects

CREATE YOUR DISPLAY TO BE REALISTIC AND ACHIEVABLE!

1) View it frequently.
2) Repeat affirmations aloud to friends, family, and most importantly, yourself.
3) Add to your display frequently; you and your life are positive works in progress.
4) It is okay to change things or alter the goal action.

Make your hopes and dreams come true.

Affirmations at Work

FOR THE FACILITATOR

I. Purpose

To use positive affirmations, images, and actions to maximize individual potential.

II. Skills

Define and describe positive affirmations.

State seven or more components of effective affirmations.

Identify six or more ways to use positive affirmations.

Compose one affirmation.

Compose three additional affirmations with their accompanying actions.

III. Possible Activities

a. If possible have display materials, magazines, scissors and glue available for teens to start their *My Affirmations and More* displays.

b. Distribute the three handouts

Affirmations at Work, page 15.

Affirmations at Work: What is More?, page 16.

Volunteers read the information aloud and discuss concepts.

Teens compose affirmations, actions, share, and receive peer feedback.

Affirmations at Work: Put It All Together, page 17.

Volunteers read the information aloud and discuss concepts.

Teens begin their displays or display plans, and then share and receive peer feedback.

IV. Enrichment Activities

a. Teens create a *Group Affirmations and More* display.

b. Teens use the group members as accountability partners with whom they can review affirmations and actions toward goals.

Either Way, You're Right!

Whether you think you can, or whether you
think you can't — you're right.

~ Henry Ford

What you think, turns into self-talk or affirmations.
Affirmations can be positive or negative.

Place the letters for each affirmation into the corresponding person's thought bubble.

A. I can't do it.

B. I learn from my mistakes.

C. I will never be good enough.

D. I am willing to try.

E. I mess up every time.

F. I make my own luck.

G. I always do the wrong thing.

H. I don't expect life to always be fair.

I. I'm unlucky.

J. I can do it!

K. It's not fair.

L. My best is good enough.

LIKELY TO NOT TRY OR TO GIVE-UP

LIKELY TO DO MY BEST

Think about the aspect of life that matters most to you.

Create your own affirmation.

LIKELY TO DO MY BEST

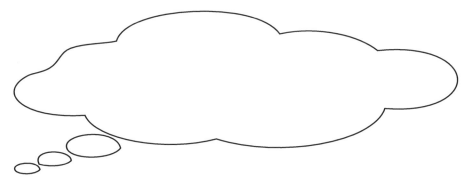

Either Way, You're Right!
FOR THE FACILITATOR

I. Purpose
To recognize that thoughts can become either positive or negative affirmations.
To acknowledge the power of positive thoughts and affirmations.

II. Skills
Discuss the power of positive and negative thoughts conveyed by a quotation.
Give examples of how thoughts have affected own performance.
Differentiate between negative and positive affirmations by completing the following:
> Placing six negative affirmations into the "LIKELY TO NOT TRY OR TO GIVE-UP" thought bubble.
> Placing six positive affirmations in the "LIKELY TO DO MY BEST" thought bubble.

Compose a positive affirmation for the aspect of life that matters most to the teen.

III. Possible Activities
a. Distribute the *Either Way, You're Right!* handout.
b. Volunteers read the quotation and directions aloud.
c. Teens discuss the quotation and give examples of how their thoughts influenced their performance.
d. Teens complete the activity and share their responses.

Answer key
LIKELY TO NOT TRY OR TO GIVE-UP
> A C E G I K

LIKELY TO DO MY BEST
> B D F H J L

e. Ask, "Do any of the statements sound like people you know?"
f. Ask, "How does hearing those positive and negative statements affect you?"
g. Teens compose their own affirmation; share aloud.
h. Teens cut out the affirmations and post them in a prominent place (wallet, mirror, computer, *My Affirmations and More* display, etc.).

IV. Enrichment Activities
Individuals or teams research and report to the group:
- Findings about the value of positive thoughts and affirmations.
- Positive thoughts and affirmations quotations.

THE POSITIVE EQUATION = THOUGHTS

You can think your way into positive or negative actions!

Thoughts + Affirmations = Actions

Give three examples to show how your negative thoughts and affirmations can influence actions.

Negative Thoughts +	Negative Affirmations =	Negative Actions
Ex: I'll never make any friends in this new school.	*Ex: Nobody ever likes me.*	*Ex: I avoid trying to make friends.*

Give three examples to show how your positive thoughts and affirmations can influence actions.

Positive Thoughts +	Positive Affirmations =	Positive Actions
Ex: I can make friends.	*Ex: I have likeable qualities.*	*Ex: I can smile and talk to people.*

THE POSITIVE EQUATION = PROCESS

Thoughts, affirmations, and actions need to focus on the process, not the outcome. The process is what you can control.

Give three examples and reasons why each is unrealistic.

Outcome Thought	Outcome Affirmation	Outcome Action	Unrealistic Because ...
Example: *I will win the election.*	*Example:* *I am class president.*	*Example:* *Tell everyone "I'll win."*	*Example:* *In the end, I can't control how people vote.*

Give three examples and reasons why each is realistic.

Process Thought	Process Affirmation	Process Action	Realistic Because ...
Example: *I would be a good class president.*	*Example:* *I'm running a great campaign.*	*Example:* *I speak about issues and solutions.*	*Example:* *I can try my best to win. If I don't win, I will know that I really tried!*

THE POSITIVE EQUATION = ACTIONS

You can act your way into positive thinking!

Example:
   You know you can be hot tempered, and right now, you are very upset.
   You walk away to cool off even though you want to lash out.
   You later think "I can control my anger."

Draw yourself taking a positive action when you feel like doing something negative.

My new positive thought about myself is ...

_____

_____

_____

THE POSITIVE EQUATION

FOR THE FACILITATOR

I. Purpose

To recognize that thoughts and affirmations affect actions, and likewise, actions affect thoughts and affirmations.

II. Skills

Compose six examples to show how thoughts and affirmations affect actions.
Give three examples of outcome and process statements.
Explain why each statement is unrealistic or realistic.
Draw self, taking positive action despite negative feelings.
Journal the thought resulting from the positive action.

III. Possible Activities

a.   Distribute *The Positive Equation – Thoughts* handout, page 21.
b.   Volunteers read the information, directions, and examples aloud.
c.   Teens complete the activity, share responses, and receive peer feedback.
d.   Repeat the above steps for these pages.
     The Positive Equation - Process, page 22,
     and
     The Positive Equation - Actions, page 23.

IV. Enrichment activities

Teens discuss ways to apply the concepts to their past and present experiences, and to future goals.

TRAITS/QUALITIES ②

*I can tell you character traits I admire and work to develop in myself —
perseverance, self-discipline, courage to stand up for what's right,
even when it's against one's friends or one's self.*

~ Dalia Mogahed

Take-Away Skills

Conditions and Behavior (1), *Frequency and Duration* (2), and/or *Accomplishment* (3) statements for each activity may be used in educational and/or treatment planning, and also used to measure progress toward goals. These Take-Away skills promote real life outcomes and behavioral changes.

EXAMPLES

1. *Conditions and Behavior* – a skill or healthy habit to replace a previous less effective behavior or habit.
   - Now, I … *(less effective or undesired behavior).*
   - When I … *(when do I do this?),*
     instead I will … *(more effective or desired new behavior)* in _____ out of _____ opportunities.
2. **Frequency and Duration** – a skill or healthy habit not necessarily tied to a condition or previous behavior.
   - I will *(describe the behavior)* _____ times per _____.
3. **Accomplishment** – an outcome that is a one-time accomplishment.
   - I will *(describe the accomplishment)* by _____ *(date).*

CHAPTER 2 - Traits/Qualities
Take-Away Skills Examples

CHAPTER 2 - Traits/Qualities
Take-Away Skills Examples

Accomplishment
- *I will watch a movie about a person who has improved people's lives within the next month.*

Frequency and Duration
- *I will portray one of those new positive traits at home, one time daily, for one week.*

Conditions and Behavior
- Now, I … *choose to be with people who laugh at others.*
- When I … *decide with whom to spend time,*
  instead I will … *hang out with people who help others.*

Frequency and Duration
- *I will demonstrate a positive trait of someone whom I admire, once daily, for the next 5 days.*

Frequency and Duration
- *I will comment on social media about a humanitarian once a week for 6 weeks.*

Conditions and Behavior
- Now, I … *joke about celebrities who get in trouble.*
- When I … *want attention,*
  instead I will … *talk about a public person's charitable work, in 5 out of 5 opportunities.*

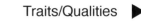

A-Z Positive Traits/Qualities

Name _____

Focusing on positive characteristics in self and others improves self-image and relationships.

Place a star in front of five or more traits you currently possess.
Place a check mark in front of five or more traits you would like to develop.
Place a question mark in front of five or more traits you are unsure about possessing or developing.

Accessible	Consistent	Good-natured	Nurturing	Sincere
Accountable	Contemplative	Gracious	Open-minded	Skillful
Active	Contributor	Grateful	Optimistic	Sociable
Adaptable	Cooperative	Hardworking	Organized	Solid
Adventurous	Coping	Healthy	Patient	Spiritual
Advocate	Courageous	Helpful	Peaceful	Spontaneous
Agreeable	Creative	Honest	Perceptive	Stable
Ambitious	Curious	Honorable	Planner	Stress manager
Amiable	Decisive	Humble	Pleasant	Strong
Appreciative	Dedicated	Humorous	Polite	Studious
Appropriate	Dependable	Imaginative	Powerful	Successful
Articulate	Determined	Independent	Practical	Supportive
Aspiring	Disciplined	Individualistic	Principled	Sympathetic
Assertive	Discreet	Initiator	Proactive	Tactful
Astute	Dynamic	Innovative	Problem-solver	Talented
Attentive	Educated	Inquiring	Productive	Team player
Authentic	Effective	Insightful	Progressive	Thorough
Aware	Efficient	Intelligent	Proud	Time manager
Balanced	Empathetic	Interested	Punctual	Tolerant
Brave	Energetic	Interesting	Rational	Trusting
Calm	Enthusiastic	Intuitive	Realistic	Trustworthy
Candid	Ethical	Joyful	Reflective	Truthful
Capable	Expressive	Kind	Reliable	Uncomplaining
Caring	Fair	Knowledgeable	Resourceful	Understanding
Charitable	Faithful	Leader	Respectful	Venturesome
Cheerful	Flexible	Listener	Responsible	Versatile
Clear-headed	Focused	Lively	Role-model	Vibrant
Collaborator	Forgiving	Logical	Secure	Warm
Communicator	Friendly	Lovable	Self-aware	Well-read
Compassionate	Fun-loving	Loving	Self-confident	Well-rounded
Confident	Extraordinary	Loyal	Self-reliant	Willing
Connected	Generous	Mature	Self-sufficient	Wise
Conscientious	Gentle	Moderate	Sensitive	Zealous
Considerate	Genuine	Neat	Sentimental	other _____

AFFIRMATIONS

Example:	My Own Affirmation ...	My Action ...
I believe in the power of affirmations		

A-Z Traits/Qualities

FOR THE FACILITATOR

I. Purpose

To recognize, exemplify, and develop positive traits/qualities. To define unfamiliar traits/qualities. To retain a working list of positive traits to refer to during upcoming activities.

II. Skills

Define unfamiliar traits.

Identify five or more traits/qualities currently possessed.

Name five or more traits/qualities to develop.

Discuss traits/qualities teens are unsure about possessing or developing.

Share personal examples of currently possessed traits in action.

Brainstorm ways to develop desired traits/qualities.

Compose an affirmation with its accompanying action.

Create acrostics using the letters in one or more traits/qualities.

III. Possible Activities

a. Distribute the *A-Z Positive Traits/Qualities* handout.
b. Volunteers read the information, directions and lists aloud and discuss concepts.
c. Volunteers name traits/qualities that are unfamiliar.
d. Volunteers define those traits/qualities and/or research and share the definitions.
e. Allow time for completion.
f. Teens share traits/qualities they currently possess and those they want to develop.
g. Teens discuss reasons they are unsure about possessing or developing question-marked traits/qualities.
h. Teens share examples of their currently possessed traits/qualities in action.
i. Teens brainstorm ways to develop desired traits/qualities.
j. A volunteer reads the affirmation aloud at the bottom left of the page.
k. Teens compose their own affirmation with its accompanying action; share aloud.
l. Teens cut out the affirmations and post them in prominent places (wallet, mirror, computer, *My Affirmations and More* display, etc.)
m. Teens keep the list of *A-Z Positive Traits/Qualities* for later reference, or facilitator collects them, to distribute when using the following handouts:
   Wallpaper, page 31, *Positive Traits Skit*, page 35, *Positive People I Know*, page 38.

IV. Enrichment Activities

Encourage individuals or teams to select a trait/quality and compose an acrostic, using the letters in the word to begin each line.

Examples:

WARM
   W elcome others with open arms,
   A cceptance and affection.
   R ecognize their value.
   M ake sure to smile

LEADER
   L isten
   E nergize
   A dvocate
   D elegate
   E ducate
   R espect

I Am Proactive!

Wallpaper Affirmations

**Adopt a trait you'd be proud to possess in the future
with a message you will see several times a day.**

Refer to the *A-Z Positive Traits/Qualities* list.
Choose a trait you hope to acquire.
Create a wallpaper for your computer, cell phone, pad, book reader, etc.
Write a message on one line below.
Then pass the paper to the next person.

_____
_____
_____
_____
_____
_____
_____
_____
_____
_____
_____
_____
_____
_____
_____
_____
_____
_____
_____
_____
_____
_____
_____

AFFIRMATIONS

Example:	My Own Affirmation …	My Action …
Be the energizer bunny!		*Use it as my wallpaper.*

Wallpaper Affirmations
FOR THE FACILITATOR

I. Purpose
To be reminded of a desired positive trait/quality several times daily.

II. Skills
Identify a positive trait/quality one would like to adopt.

Compose a message to be used as wallpaper on one's computer, cell phone, pad, book reader, etc.

Select one's own message or a peer's message to use on a computer, cell phone, pad, book reader, etc.

Research, record, and share, inspirational quotations to use as wallpaper.

III. Possible Activities
a. Teens discuss what they currently see on their computer screensaver or smartphone wallpaper.

b. Teens estimate the number of times they look at their computer/phone screens daily.

c. Read the *Wallpaper Affirmations* handout information and directions aloud to the teens.

d. Refer teens to the *A-Z Positive Trait/Quality* list, page 29.

e. Distribute one copy of the *Wallpaper Affirmations* handout to the first teen.

f. Each teen writes a number message and passes the paper.

g. The messages are shared in one of the following ways:
   - Volunteers read the messages aloud as other volunteers write them on the board.
   - Teens copy them onto notebook paper.
   - The list is photocopied and distributed to all.

h. Teens privately circle their favorite messages and plan to use them on their computer, cell phone, pad, book reader, etc.

IV. Enrichment Activities
Teens research, record, and share inspirational quotations to use as wallpaper on computer, cell phone, pad, book reader, etc.

Positive Traits Match Game

Your traits are distinguishing qualities that belong to you or that you can acquire. Positive traits draw people to you.

✂ TRAITS	DESCRIPTIONS	✂ TRAITS	DESCRIPTIONS
Curious	Inquisitive; interested in the world.	**Cautious**	Careful to avoid dangers to self and others.
Open-minded	Non-judgmental; examine all sides.	**Humble**	Unpretentious; not seeking the spotlight.
Courageous	Brave; face fears; take on challenges.	**Grateful**	Thankful; appreciate what people do or give.
Diligent	Persistent; stick to the task.	**Optimistic**	Hopeful; see the glass as half full.
Honest	Trustworthy, speak the truth.	**Spiritual**	Believe in a higher purpose and meaning of the universe.
Kind	Caring; consider interests of others.	**Forgiving**	Pardon people for wrongdoing.
Generous	Give time, talents, and resources.	**Humor**	See the funny side of situations; help others laugh.
Loyal	Faithful to family and friends; dedicated to teammates.	**Passionate**	Enthusiastic; put heart, mind, whole self into an activity.
Leadership	Organize activities; guide others toward group goals.	**Resilient**	Strong; quick to bounce back.
Self-control	Regulate own emotions and actions.	**Authentic**	Genuine; show real self.

AFFIRMATIONS

Example:	My Own Affirmation …	My Action …
I use my positive traits daily.		

Positive Traits Match Game

FOR THE FACILITATOR

I. Purpose

To describe and give examples of positive traits.

II. Skills

Match twenty positive traits with their descriptions.
Give examples of traits and guess traits based on peers' examples.
Compose an affirmation with its accompanying action.

III. Possible Activities

Before the session decide on the individual or interactive game.

Individual Game

- Photocopy two of the *Positive Traits Match Game* handouts per participant.
- Distribute one handout to each teen and have scissors available. (Retain the second copies).
- Teens cut out the boxes and scramble the cutouts and match "traits" (cutout in bold letters) with "descriptions" (larger cutout) in columns.
- Teens then share their matches.
- Distribute the second copies for the answer key and affirmations.

Interactive Game

- Photocopy one *Positive Traits Match Game* handout per participant and one extra, (for cutouts).
- Cut out the boxes on the extra photocopy. (Retain the uncut copies).
- Place "traits" (one word in bold letters) in one stack; "descriptions" (larger cutout) in another stack.
- Distribute trait cutouts to half of the group members.
- Distribute description cutouts to the other half of the group members.
- Teens take turns. One at a time they do the following:
  Go to the front of the room and read a "trait" or "description" aloud.
  The teens with the matching traits or descriptions read their cutouts aloud.
- Distribute the uncut copies for the answer key and affirmations.

Both Individual and Interactive Game Formats

a. Refer teens to the uncut copies of the handout.
b. A volunteer reads the affirmation aloud at the bottom left of the page.
c. Teens compose their own affirmation with its accompanying action; share aloud.
d. Teens cut out the affirmations and post them in prominent places (wallet, mirror, computer, *My Affirmations and More* display, etc.)

IV. Enrichment Activities

Play "Guess the Trait."

- Teens share one sentence scenarios that exemplify a trait, without saying the word.
- Peers guess the trait. Example scenario: *A sophomore was given too much change, told the cashier, and returned the extra money. Guess the Trait – Honesty.*

Positive Traits Skits

**Create a skit to portray six or more positive traits.
Actors do not need scripts. They will improvise!**

Setting

_____

_____

_____

_____

Characters

_____

_____

_____

_____

Plot *(ideas about positive traits and how the characters will portray them)*

_____

_____

_____

_____

_____

_____

_____

_____

_____

_____

_____

_____

_____

AFFIRMATIONS

Example:	My Own Affirmation …	My Action …
I recognize positive traits in others.		

Positive Traits Skits
FOR THE FACILITATOR

I. Purpose
To convey positive traits through skits.

II. Skills
Collaborate with peers to create and enact a skit showing six or more positive traits.

List six or more positive traits shown in peers' skits.

Compose an affirmation with its accompanying action.

Identify characters in literature, movies, and television who portray positive traits.

III. Possible Activities
a. Distribute the *Positive Traits Skits* handout.

b. Refer teens to the *A-Z Positive Traits/Qualities* list, page 29.

c. Volunteers read the directions aloud.

d. The group separates into small teams, whose members write and act in short skits.
    Option – create friendly competition in which the skit showing the most positive traits wins.

e. Teens write notes on their handouts, and rehearse in different corners of the room.

f. The group re-convenes.

g. Teams take turns performing; other teams become audience members.

h. Audience members list the positive traits they observe.

i. After each performance, teens discuss the traits portrayed and observed.

j. Teens process how they felt as they created, performed, and viewed the skits.

k. A volunteer reads the affirmation aloud at the bottom left of the page.

l. Teens compose their own affirmation with its accompanying action; share aloud.

m. Teens cut out the affirmations and post them in prominent places (wallet, mirror, computer, *My Affirmations and More* display, etc.).

IV. Enrichment Activities
Teens discuss characters who portray positive traits in literature, movies, and television.

Positive People I Know

**Think about friends, family, teachers, and others, and complete the columns below.
Use code names. *Example: If your friend Loves To Swim, use LTS.***

People I Know	Their Positive Traits	How they Show their Traits
Ex: My best friend	*Ex: Loyalty*	*Ex. Defends me if people gossip*
1.	1.	1.
2.	2.	2.
3.	3.	3.
4.	4.	4.
5.	5.	5.

AFFIRMATIONS

Example:	My Own Affirmation …	My Action …
I surround myself with positive people.		

Positive People I Know
FOR THE FACILITATOR

I. Purpose
To identify people with positive traits.

II. Skills
Identify five personally known people who exemplify a positive trait.
State each person's trait and how it is demonstrated.
Compose an affirmation with its accompanying action.
Identify one or more and ways to personally exemplify traits admired in others.

III. Possible Activities
a. Distribute the *Positive People I Know* handout.
b. Refer teens to the *A-Z Positive Traits/Qualities* list, page 29.
c. Volunteers read the directions aloud.
d. Teens complete and share their lists, and receive peer feedback.
e. A volunteer reads the affirmation aloud at the bottom left of the page.
f. Teens compose their own affirmation with its accompanying action; share aloud.
g. Teens cut out the affirmations and post them in prominent places (wallet, mirror, computer, *My Affirmations and More* display, etc.).

IV. Enrichment Activity
Teens discuss ways they can exemplify the traits they admire in others.

Suggestion – follow up with the *Journalist for a Day* handout, page 39, in which teens will identify pop culture examples of positive traits.

Journalist for a Day

Imagine you are a television broadcast journalist preparing a human interest story for tonight's six o'clock evening news show.

Think about a positive role-model in pop culture. Consider how the person has helped the world. Research and report facts. Share what you know about the person. Focus on the person's positive traits and actions. You may volunteer to read your article to your TV viewers.

Prepare your teleprompter text in the space below.

_____

_____

_____

_____

_____

_____

_____

_____

_____

_____

_____

If you had the ability to give everyone in the world one trait, what would it be?

_____

_____

Explain_____

_____

_____

AFFIRMATIONS

Example:	My Own Affirmation …	My Action …
I choose to admire positive role models.		

Journalist for a Day
FOR THE FACILITATOR

I. Purpose
To emulate positive traits and behaviors of pop culture icons.

II. Skills
Identify people from entertainment and/or sports that teens admire.
Research and report facts about the person's actions.
Identify the trait one would like to give the world.
Reverse negative news stories with positive substitutions.
Compose an affirmation with its accompanying action.

III. Possible Activities
a. Teens discuss whether good or bad news receives more media attention and why.
b. Teens brainstorm some elements of a human interest story:
- Emotional content
- Descriptions of people and places
- Direct quotations
- Who, What, When, Where, Why, and How, and Who Said So?
- Humor

c. Distribute the *Journalist for a Day* handout.
d. Volunteers read the directions aloud.
e. Teens complete the teleprompter text.
f. Volunteers sit at the front of the room, read their news clips, and receive peer feedback.
g. Volunteers share their responses to the questions under the teleprompter text.
h. A volunteer reads the affirmation aloud at the bottom left of the page.
i. Teens compose their own affirmation with its accompanying action; share aloud.
j. Teens cut out the affirmations and post them in prominent places (wallet, mirror, computer, *My Affirmations and More* display, etc.).

IV. Enrichment Activities
a. Teens discuss ways to promote the positive traits they would like to give the world.
b. Teens recall recent negative news about people in the public eye.
c. Teens substitute positive news stories orally or by writing on the board.
Substitutions may be fictional, humorous, or reality-based.
Example:
Negative news – "Joined in a protest rally, and destroyed and looted property."
Positive substitution – "Joined in a protest rally and worked very hard to keep fellow protesters calm and obeying the curfews."

CHALLENGES ③

I don't run away from a challenge because I'm afraid. Instead, I run toward it because the only way to escape the fear is to trample it beneath your feet.

~ Nadia Comaneci

Take-Away Skills

Conditions and Behavior (1), *Frequency and Duration* (2), and/or *Accomplishment* (3) statements for each activity may be used in educational and/or treatment planning, and also used to measure progress toward goals. These Take-Away skills promote real life outcomes and behavioral changes.

EXAMPLES

1. *Conditions and Behavior* – a skill or healthy habit to replace a previous less effective behavior or habit.
   - Now, I … *(less effective or undesired behavior)*.
   - When I … *(when do I do this?)*,
     instead I will … *(more effective or desired new behavior)* in _____ out of _____ opportunities.
2. **Frequency and Duration** – a skill or healthy habit not necessarily tied to a condition or previous behavior.
   - I will *(describe the behavior)* _____ times per _____.
3. **Accomplishment** – an outcome that is a one-time accomplishment.
   - I will *(describe the accomplishment)* by _____ *(date)*.

CHAPTER 3 - Challenges
Take-Away Skills Examples

Accomplishment
   - *I will identify one aspect of emotional growth to work on by September 30th.*
Frequency and Duration
   - *I will journal my progress toward that aspect of growth once weekly for 4 weeks.*
Conditions and Behavior
   - Now, I … *say "This is terrible!"*
   - When I … *am in a difficult situation,*
     instead I will … *say "This is part of maturity!" in 5 out of 5 opportunities.*
Conditions and Behavior
   - Now, I … *give up when people say "It can't be done."*
   - When I … *want to achieve a goal,*
     instead I will … *take steps to find out for myself if it can be done, in 4 out of 5 opportunities.*
Conditions and Behavior
   - Now, I … *keep talking about past actions I regret.*
   - When I … *feel guilty,*
     instead I will … *talk about the lessons I have learned, in 3 out of 5 opportunities.*

CHAPTER 3 - Challenges
Take-Away Skills Examples

    Conditions and Behavior
- Now, I … *say, "My whole life is ruined forever."*
- When I … *discuss a disappointment,*
  instead I will … *say, "This is temporary, in 5 out of 5 opportunities.*

    Accomplishment
- *I will help comfort someone who has had a disappointment within the week.*

    Accomplishment
- *I will post an opinion about an issue important to me by October 1st.*

    Conditions and Behavior
- Now, I … *keep quiet about my beliefs.*
- When I … *hear people express opposing beliefs,*
  instead I will … *assertively express my beliefs in 5 out of 5 opportunities.*

GROWTH — CYCLE

For a seed to achieve its greatest expression,
it must come completely undone.
The shell cracks, its insides come out and everything changes.
To someone who doesn't understand growth,
it would look like complete destruction.

~ Cynthia Occelli

Jot down how you think each stage contributed to your emotional growth.

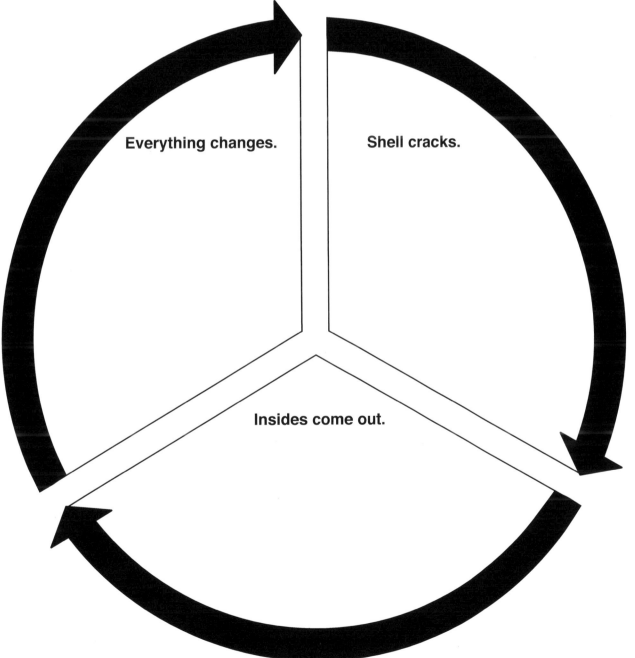

Everything changes.

Shell cracks.

Insides come out.

GROWTH – THOUGHTS

For a seed to achieve its greatest expression,
it must come completely undone.
The shell cracks, its insides come out and everything changes.
To someone who doesn't understand growth,
it would look like complete destruction.

~ Cynthia Occelli

Write your thoughts as you respond to these comparisons.

Within a seed is the ability for growth.
What, within you, guides your ability to grow emotionally?

_____

_____

Roots anchor the seed.
What are your roots that keep you stable emotionally?

_____

_____

Seeds need water and minerals for nourishment and growth.
What nourishes you emotionally?

_____

_____

Some plants need fertilizer to grow, even if it smells bad.
What seems distasteful to you but helps you grow emotionally?

_____

_____

Many plants need *light*.
What *enlightens* and inspires you?

_____

_____

AFFIRMATIONS

Example:	My Own Affirmation …	My Action …
I am growing emotionally.		

GROWTH – A SEED

For a seed to achieve its greatest expression,
it must come completely undone.
The shell cracks,
its insides come out and everything changes.
To someone who doesn't understand growth,
it would look like complete destruction.

~ Cynthia Occelli

What situation in your life has contributed to your emotional growth?

My Growth

GROWTH
FOR THE FACILITATOR

I. Purpose
To recognize that what often looks like destruction is emotional growth.

II. Skills
Draw and/or describe personal growth related to a quotation about a seed.
Identify comparisons between emotional growth and a seed in each of the following ways:

Shell cracks	Instructions for growth	Fertilizer
Insides come out	Roots	Light
Everything changes	Nourishment	

Compose an affirmation with its accompanying action.

III. Possible Activities
a. Distribute each of the *Growth* handouts one at a time.
b. Complete each before distributing the next.

Growth – Cycle, page 45.
Team Format
> Teens form three teams (shell cracks, insides come out, everything changes).
> Each team brainstorms and documents ideas.
> The group reconvenes, teams share their responses, and receive peer feedback.

Board Activity Format
> Facilitator or volunteer copies the diagram on the board, leads brainstorming, and lists ideas.

Individual Format
> Teens complete the activity, share their ideas, and receive peer feedback.

Growth – Thoughts, page 46.
Panel Format
> A volunteer reads the questions aloud and volunteers respond.

Individual Format
> Teens complete the activity, share their responses, and receive peer feedback.

Growth – A Seed, page 47.
> A volunteer reads the quotation and instructions aloud.
> Teens draw and/or describe their emotional growth, share, and receive peer feedback.

c. A volunteer reads the affirmation aloud at the bottom left of the page.
d. Teens compose their own affirmation with its accompanying action; share aloud.
e. Teens cut out the affirmations and post them in prominent places (wallet, mirror, computer, *My Affirmations and More* display, etc.).

IV. Enrichment Activities
Teens brainstorm the essentials for emotional growth (honesty with self/others, support, faith, resilience, and willingness to ask for and receive help, etc.).

Yay-Sayer versus Nay-Sayer

A Nay-Sayer expresses negative or pessimistic views.

A Yay-Sayer expresses positive or optimistic views.

Write a limerick about what it takes to be a Yay-Sayer.

A limerick is a five-line poem with the rhyme scheme AABBA.

Example:
The Breakup

There once was a couple whose breakup
Was actually cause for a wake-up.
People said, "You got burned!"
Yet both of them learned,
"We've glimpsed love and loss close-up".

Title of My Limerick _____

_____

_____

_____

_____

_____

_____

_____

_____

AFFIRMATIONS

Example:	**My Own Affirmation …**	**My Action …**
I say "can" when others say "I can't."		

Yay-Sayer versus Nay-Sayer
FOR THE FACILITATOR

I. Purpose
To view a potentially negative event in a positive light.

II. Skills
State the definition of *Nay-Sayer* and the made-up word *Yay-Sayer*.
Counteract negativity through a limerick that includes the following:
    Description of what a Nay-Sayer might say and a description of what a Yay-Sayer might say.
Recognize three or more sensible precautions and state them in positive ways.
Compose an affirmation with its accompanying action.

III. Possible Activities
a. Distribute the *Yay-Sayer* versus *Nay-Sayer* handout.
b. Volunteers read the information, directions and example aloud.
c. Teens identify the Nay-Sayer comment in the limerick ("You got burned!").
d. Teens identify the Yay-Sayer response ("We've glimpsed love and loss close-up.")
e. Individuals or teams create and share limericks, and receive peer feedback.
f. A volunteer reads the affirmation at the bottom left of the page.
g. Teens compose their own affirmation with its accompanying action; share aloud.
h. Teens cut out the affirmations and post them in prominent places (wallet, mirror, computer, *My Affirmations and More* display, etc.).

IV. Enrichment Activity
a. Teens brainstorm sensible precautions and then state them in positive terms.
b. A volunteer lists ideas on the board.
Examples
"Don't text and drive" also means *"Give your full attention to the road."*
"Don't gossip" also means *"Talk about people's positive traits."*
"Don't procrastinate" also means *"Do it now and reward yourself afterward."*

The Past

Dwelling on past negative incidents can prevent positive thinking.

The past is smoke. When necessary blow it away.

~ Ralph B. Binyen

1. Complete the thought below.
2. Draw swirls of smoke next to the thought.
3. Imagine yourself blowing the thought away.

A part of my past to blow away is …

_____

_____

_____

1. Complete the thought below.
2. Draw a heart next to the thought.
3. Imagine keeping the thought in your heart forever.

A part of my past to always remember is …

_____

_____

_____

1. Complete the thought below.
2. Draw a brain next to the thought.
3. Imagine the thought's impact on your life.

A part of my past to learn from is …

_____

_____

_____

AFFIRMATIONS

Example:	My Own Affirmation …	My Action …
I decide what to value in my past and what to blow away.		

The Past
FOR THE FACILITATOR

I. Purpose
To stop dwelling on past negativity, cherish positive memories, and gain insight from the past.

II. Skills
Use journaling, drawing, and imagery to describe parts of the past to illustrate the following:
Dismiss
Remember
Learn from
Compose an affirmation with its accompanying action.
Create six word slogans about the past.

III. Possible Activities
a. Distribute *The Past* handout.
b. Volunteers read the information, quotation, and directions aloud.
c. Teens complete the activity, share their responses, and receive peer feedback.
d. A volunteer reads the affirmation aloud at the bottom left of the page.
e. Teens compose their own affirmation with its accompanying action; share aloud.
f. Teens cut out the affirmations and post them in prominent places (wallet, mirror, computer, *My Affirmations and More* display, etc.).

IV. Enrichment Activities
Individuals or teams create and share "Say it in six words" slogans about the past.
Examples:
- *It happened there, leave it there.*
- *Memories may be sweet or bittersweet.*
- *Amazing lessons are learned from mistakes.*

Personal? Permanent? Pervasive? NOT!

Personal = relating to you
Permanent = continuing forever
Pervasive = spreading through every part of your life

Fill in the columns with thoughts about two disappointing situations.

My disappointing situation	My part in why it happened	It's NOT totally personal	It's NOT permanent	It's NOT pervasive
Example: I received a failing grade.	I did not study enough.	Other responsibilities interfered with studying.	I can study for future tests.	I can do well in other classes.
1.				
2.				

AFFIRMATIONS

Example: I see disappointments as temporary.	My Own Affirmation …	My Action …

Personal? Permanent? Pervasive? NOT!
FOR THE FACILITATOR

I. Purpose
To take responsibility for one's personal role in disappointments.
To acknowledge external factors, aspects that are temporary, and outcomes that are confined to one situation.

II. Skills
Identify a disappointing situation.
Describe the following:
> A personal role or responsibility
> External factors
> Ways to make the situation temporary
> How to prevent it from happening in other situations

Compose an affirmation with its accompanying action.
Discuss ways to find comfort when disappointing situations seem permanent.

III. Possible Activities
a. Distribute the *Personal? Permanent? Pervasive? NOT!* handout.
b. Volunteers read the definitions, directions, and example aloud.
c. Teens complete their situations, share their responses, and receive peer feedback.
d. A volunteer reads the affirmation aloud at the bottom left of the page.
e. Teens compose their own affirmation with its accompanying action; share aloud.
f. Teens cut out the affirmations and post them in prominent places (wallet, mirror, computer, *My Affirmations and More* display, etc.).

IV. Enrichment Activities
a. Teens brainstorm disappointing situations that are permanent.
   Examples: death of a loved one, loss of a limb, parental divorce, etc.
b. Teens discuss ways to find comfort.
   Possibilities
   - A loved one is gone, and a support system is present.
   - A limb can be replaced by a prosthesis.
   - Divorce may lead to the ability to adapt to new situations, no more fighting, a safe and a more positive environment.

Speak Your Truth

> *For good ideas and true innovation, you need human interaction, conflict, argument, debate.*
>
> ~ Margaret Heffernan

What are your thoughts about the above quotation?

_____

_____

_____

_____

Many people fear conflict. Silence can be worse.

**Write five 'truth about life' statements
that you feel passionate about and are prepared to defend.**

1. _____

_____

2. _____

_____

3. _____

_____

4. _____

_____

5. _____

_____

AFFIRMATIONS

Example:	My Own Affirmation …	My Action …
I respectfully speak my truth.		

Speak Your Truth
FOR THE FACILITATOR

I. Purpose
To speak one's truth.
To acknowledge that conflict is an important component of considering new ideas.

II. Skills
Acknowledge the value of conflict, argument and debate.
Identify five statements one is prepared to defend.
Defend one or more of the statements in the presence of opposition.
Compose an affirmation with its accompanying action.

III. Possible Activities
a. Ask for a show of hands of teens who fear conflict.
b. Ask about times when silence is worse (going along with actions against personal values, etc.).
c. Distribute the *Speak Your Truth* handout.
d. Ask teens to read the quotation in the box at the top of the page and respond on the lines below.
e. Discuss the group's thoughts regarding the quotation.
f. Teens complete their lists of five 'truth' statements.
g. If students do not have 'truth about life statements,' they might want to think about something from a movie or book that inspired them.
h. Volunteers speak their truths by reading their lists aloud.
i. A volunteer reads the affirmation aloud at the bottom left of the page.
j. Teens compose their own affirmation with its accompanying action; share aloud.
k. Teens cut out the affirmations and post them in prominent places (wallet, mirror, computer, *My Affirmations and More* display, etc.).

IV. Enrichment Activities
Volunteers defend the statements on their lists through discussion and debate.

THOUGHT RE-PROGRAMMING 4

*Nurture your mind with great thoughts,
for you will never go any higher than you think.*

~ Benjamin Disraeli

Take-Away Skills

Conditions and Behavior (1), *Frequency and Duration* (2), and/or *Accomplishment* (3) statements for each activity may be used in educational and/or treatment planning, and also used to measure progress toward goals. These Take-Away skills promote real life outcomes and behavioral changes.

EXAMPLES

1. *Conditions and Behavior* – a skill or healthy habit to replace a previous less effective behavior or habit.
   - Now, I … *(less effective or undesired behavior)*.
   - When I … *(when do I do this?)*,
     instead I will … *(more effective or desired new behavior)* in _____ out of _____ opportunities.
2. **Frequency and Duration** – a skill or healthy habit not necessarily tied to a condition or previous behavior.
   - I will *(describe the behavior)* _____ times per _____.
3. **Accomplishment** – an outcome that is a one-time accomplishment.
   - I will *(describe the accomplishment)* by _____ *(date)*.

CHAPTER 4 - Thought Re-programming
Take-Away Skills Examples

CHAPTER 4 - Thought Re-programming
Take-Away Skills Examples

TRASH DISTORTED THOUGHTS

Your distorted thoughts can make you miserable.

Check the boxes below to indicate the distorted thoughts you have experienced.

☐ Believing one can change others
☐ Blaming self and/or others
☐ Exaggerating a setback
☐ Labeling self and/or others
☐ Seeing the glass as half empty, i.e., focusing on what's lacking or negative
☐ Taking everything personally
☐ Thinking in extremes, such as always, never, right, wrong, etc.

Prepare for the Trash Distorted Thoughts Game.
In the trash can below, write a negative thought that has troubled you.
Do not write your name.

AFFIRMATIONS

Example:	My Own Affirmation …	My Action …
My thoughts become my reality.		

TRASH DISTORTED THOUGHTS
FOR THE FACILITATOR

I. Purpose
To recognize distorted thoughts.
To replace distorted thoughts with positive but realistic alternatives.

II. Skills
Identify types of thought distortions experienced.
Give examples of thought distortions.
Identify a personally troubling thought.
Replace distorted thoughts with positive but realistic alternatives.
Compose an affirmation with its accompanying action.

III. Possible Activities
a. Distribute the *Trash Distorted Thoughts* handout.
b. Volunteers read the directions and checklist aloud.
c. Teens give examples of the distortions.
d. Teens complete the checklists.
e. Teens write troublesome thoughts on their trash can picture.
f. Teens cut out the trash can pictures.
g. Cutouts are placed in a stack at the front of the room.
h. A trash can or wastebasket is placed within a challenging distance from the front of the room.

The Trash Distorted Thoughts Game Play
In each turn, a teen goes to the front of the room and …
- Picks up a trash can cutout
- Reads the distorted thought aloud
- Calls on volunteers who state positive but realistic alternatives
- Crumples and tosses the cutout, aiming to land it into the trash can

i. A volunteer reads the affirmation aloud at the bottom left of the page.
j. Teens compose their own affirmation with its accompanying action; share aloud.
k. Teens cut out the affirmations and post them in prominent places (wallet, mirror, computer, *My Affirmations and More* display, etc.).

IV. Enrichment Activities
Teens discuss times they have acted in these ways:
- Minimized their own positive traits
- Jumped to the worst possible conclusion
- Insisted on what self/others "should" do

Fix Your Glitch

Your mind, like a computer, can be re-programmed.

Write a negative thought (glitch) that bothers you. _____

_____

_____

Below, respond to the five re-programming tips. For each, refer to your above response.

1. **Perform a reality check.** Ask yourself and trusted people about the pros and cons of your situation.

_____

_____

2. **Write what you would say** to your best friend in the same situation.

_____

_____

3. **Replace extreme words** with less hurtful terms.
   (_Ex: Replace "horrible" with "disappointing."_)

   My extreme word for my situation _____ My less hurtful word _____

4. **Replace the glitch** with a positive but realistic thought.

_____

_____

5. **Decide (but don't dwell on)** how you would productively handle an unwanted outcome.
   Example: If I fail a class, my plan is to re-take the class and seek help from a tutor, teacher or study partner.

_____

_____

AFFIRMATIONS

Example:	My Own Affirmation ...	My Action ...
I re-program my negative thoughts.		

Fix Your Glitch
FOR THE FACILITATOR

I. Purpose
To use the concept of re-programming a computer to reframe negative thoughts (glitches).

II. Skills
Identify a personal negative thought.
Document the application of five techniques to change the thought.
Compose an affirmation with its accompanying action.
Replace peer's negative thought with a positive but realistic alternative.

III. Possible Activities
a. Distribute the *Fix Your Glitch* handout.
b. Volunteers read the bold text aloud.
c. Teens complete the activity, share their responses, and receive peer feedback.
d. A volunteer reads the affirmation aloud at the bottom left of the page.
e. Teens compose their own affirmation with its accompanying action; share aloud.
f. Teens cut out the affirmations and post them in prominent places (wallet, mirror, computer, *My Affirmations and More* display, etc.).

Enrichment Activity
Play *Replace-the-Thought*
a. Teens divide into two teams – The Optimists and The Pessimists.
b. Opposing teams stand or sit in two lines facing each other.
c. As other team members watch and listen:
   - A Pessimist states a negative thought.
   - The Optimist facing the Pessimist replaces it with a positive but realistic thought.
   - After all have played, teams switch roles.
   - The new Pessimists state negative thoughts.
   - The new Optimists state replacement thoughts.

RATIONAL or IRRATIONAL?

1	2	3	4	5	6
If someone breaks up with me, it means there is something wrong with me.	I do whatever it takes to keep people happy.	I can't say "No" when asked to do anything.	Any random challenging situation can make me miserable.	People make me feel worthless.	My past actions have ruined me forever.
7	**8**	**9**	**10**	**11**	**12**
I feel that I must do everything perfectly.	I need to do what others do so I can be popular.	If I am unable to do something that is hard to do, it means I'm a failure.	I'll find the perfect job the first time.	I must never be self-serving and think about what's best for me first.	I should never feel angry.
13	*14*	*15*	*16*	*17*	*18*
Breakups are a risk in any relationship.	*I am not responsible for anyone else's happiness.*	*To say "No" allows me to say "Yes" to something else.*	*I work at having positive thoughts about challenging situations.*	*People can't affect my feelings unless I let them.*	*My past will make me a stronger person.*
19	*20*	*21*	*22*	*23*	*24*
I expect my best, rather than perfection.	*I decide what matters most to me without being influenced by others.*	*Even though I can't do something that I thought I could, it does not mean I am a failure.*	*I'll eventually find a job that works best for me.*	*I take good care of my own mental and physical health.*	*I handle my anger carefully and positively.*

AFFIRMATIONS

Example:	My Own Affirmation …	My Action …
I ask myself "Is this thought rational?"		

RATIONAL OR IRRATIONAL?
FOR THE FACILITATOR

I. Purpose
To differentiate between twelve rational and twelve irrational ideas and their effects.

II. Skills
Differentiate between twelve irrational and twelve rational ideas and their effects.
Replace twelve irrational ideas with rational ideas.
Compose an affirmation with its accompanying action.
Apply five or more rational thinking concepts to personal life.

III. Possible Activities
   a. Photocopy one *Rational or Irrational?* handout and cut out the boxes.
       Photocopy one uncut *Rational or Irrational?* handout per teen – for f. below.
   b. Put a sign IRRATIONAL on one wall in the room and RATIONAL on another wall.
   c. Ask teens the meanings of rational and irrational (realistic, unrealistic).
   d. Scramble the cutouts and distribute one per teen.
       Use any leftover cutouts for an additional round(s).
   e. Play the game "Which Wall?"
- Emphasize that players may ask each other for help any time during the game.
- Teens silently read their cutouts and stand on the applicable side of the room.
- Teens on the IRRATIONAL side:
  Read their cutouts aloud.
  State why the ideas are irrational.
  Share the feelings that would result from the ideas.
  Compose rational alternatives.
- Teens on the RATIONAL side:
  Read their cutouts aloud.
  State why the ideas are rational.
  State the feelings that would result from the ideas.

Answer Key
Numbers 1-12 are irrational. Numbers 13-24 are rational.
Numbers 13-24 are also examples of rational alternatives for Numbers 1-12.

   f. Distribute the uncut photocopies of the handout.
   g. A volunteer reads the affirmation aloud at the bottom left of the page.
   h. Teens compose their own affirmation with its accompanying action; share aloud.
   i. Teens cut out the affirmations and post them in prominent places (wallet, mirror, computer, *My Affirmations & More* display, etc.).

IV. Enrichment Activities
Teens discuss and apply the following concepts to their lives:
- Assertiveness
- Healthy risks
- Healthy selfishness
- Personal responsibility for thoughts and feelings
- Reasons to avoid people-pleasing and perfectionism

Techno-Utopianism

**Techno-Utopianism is a blend-word which
combines "Technology" with "Utopia"**

Techno-utopianism is any ideology based on the premise that advances in science and technology will eventually bring about a utopia, or at least help to fulfill one or another utopian ideal. A techno-utopia is therefore a hypothetical ideal society.

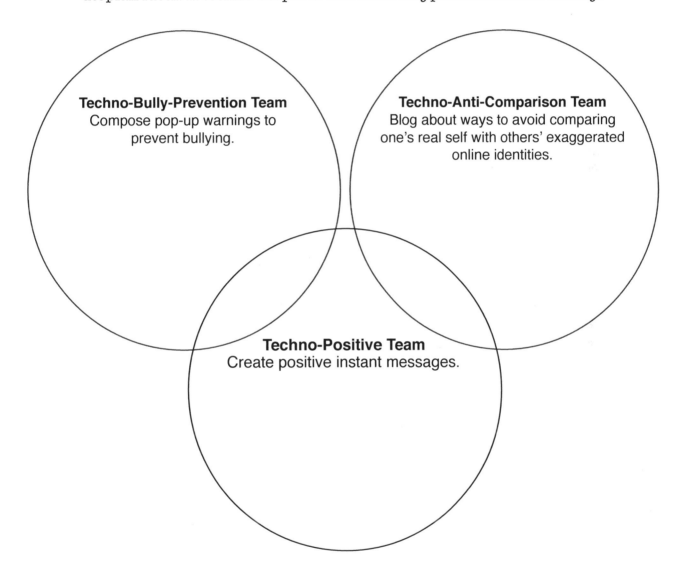

Techno-Bully-Prevention Team
Compose pop-up warnings to
prevent bullying.

Techno-Anti-Comparison Team
Blog about ways to avoid comparing
one's real self with others' exaggerated
online identities.

Techno-Positive Team
Create positive instant messages.

AFFIRMATIONS

Example:	My Own Affirmation …	My Action …
I spread only good news.		

Techno-Utopianism
FOR THE FACILITATOR

I. Purpose
To use technology for positive messages.

II. Skills
Create three or more in each category:
>   Pop-up warnings to prevent technological bullying
>   Ways to avoid comparing one's real life with others' exaggerated online identities
>   Positive instant messages

Compose an affirmation with its accompanying action.
Discuss "FOMO – Fear of Missing Out," and describe a solution.

III. Possible Activities
   a. Distribute the *Techno-Utopianism* handout.
   b. A volunteer reads the definition aloud.
   c. Teens form three teams – *Techno-Bully Prevention, Techno-Anti-Comparison* and *Techno-Positive*.
   d. Teammates confer and prepare their presentations.
   e. The group re-convenes.
   f. Teams share their responses and receive peer feedback.
   g. A volunteer reads the affirmation aloud at the bottom left of the page.
   h. Teens compose their own affirmation with its accompanying action; share aloud.
   i. Teens cut out the affirmations and post them in prominent places (wallet, mirror, computer, *My Affirmations and More* display, etc.).

Possibilities

Techno-Bully-Prevention	Techno-Anti-Comparison	Techno-Positive
Would you say it FTF? (face to face)	Know that most people do not tell the whole story online.	T+ (think positive).
Could this message hurt someone?	Volunteer to help people, then post about the fun.	All41 (all for one) – All advocate for the one being bullied.
Send AYOR (at your own risk)	Take a nature walk while AFK (away from keyboard).	Gossip is TMI (too much, or maybe false, information).

IV. Enrichment Activities
Discuss FOMA – Fear of Missing Out from focusing too much on social media.
   • Feeling pressure to be as technologically creative as others
   • Wanting to attend every party and event seen online
   • Needing to exaggerate the positive aspects of every experience
Discuss the solutions – *Ex: Spend more time **living** and less time **looking** at other people's lives.*

Common Sense

Unrealistic wishful thinking is often contrary to nature, reason, or common sense. Unrealistic wishful thinking can possibly be harmful. Wishing or imagining that something can happen might not be realistic.

Common Sense is optimism based on nature and/or reason. Common sense is essential to sound, insightful, practical judgment. It is independent of knowledge or training.

Unrealistic Wishful Thinking Example:
"I'll ace every test whether I study or not."

Common Sense Example:
"I'm likely to get better results on the test if I study."

I would like to think …	It would be helpful to think …

Unrealistic Wishful Thinking   Common Sense

AFFIRMATIONS

Example:	My Own Affirmation …	My Action …
I have common sense and I use it!		

Common Sense
FOR THE FACILITATOR

I. Purpose
To avoid potentially unrealistic wishful thinking.
To form positive thoughts based on common sense.

II. Skills
State the difference between unrealistic wishful thinking and common sense.
Formulate unrealistic wishful thoughts and their common sense alternatives.
Compose an affirmation with its accompanying action.

III. Possible Activities
a. Distribute the *Common Sense* handout.
b. Volunteers read the definitions and examples aloud.
c. Teens complete the thought boxes, share their responses, and receive peer feedback.
   Examples:
   Unrealistic Wishful Thinking – "I can smoke all I want and never get cancer."
   Common Sense – "If I don't smoke I will have a better chance at maintaining good health."
d. A volunteer reads the affirmation aloud at the bottom left of the page.
e. Teens compose their own affirmation with its accompanying action; share aloud.
f. Teens cut out the affirmations and post them in prominent places (wallet, mirror, computer, *My Affirmations and More* display, etc.).

IV. Enrichment Activities
Individually or in teams:
• Teens compose as many unrealistic wishful thoughts as they can in ten minutes.
• Teens read the thoughts aloud as peers brainstorm common sense alternatives.

CAN'T

Anonymously, write about something you would like to accomplish, but think you CAN'T.

Example:
I wish someone could tell me how I can give my opinion to people who I know will disagree with me.

✂ -

I wish someone could tell me how I can _____

_____

_____

_____

_____

_____

_____

_____

_____

_____

_____

_____

_____

_____

_____

_____

✂ -

AFFIRMATIONS

Example:	My Own Affirmation ...	My Action ...
I evaluate helpful suggestions.		

CAN'T
FOR THE FACILITATOR

Purpose

To believe a desired outcome is possible.

Skills

Identify a desired outcome that seems impossible.

Listen to peers' suggestions.

Suggest ways peers can accomplish their desired outcomes.

Compose an affirmation and its accompanying action.

Discuss helpful strategies that did not work in one situation but did or could
work in other situations.

Possible Activities

a. Distribute the *CAN'T* handout.

b. Volunteers read the information and directions aloud.

c. Teens complete the *"I wish someone could tell me how I can ..."* entry, and cut or tear their papers on the dotted lines.

d. A volunteer collects the cutouts and places them face down in the front of the room.

e. Volunteers take turns reading the cutouts aloud and encouraging peer responses.

f. Teens are directed to privately evaluate the suggestions for their entries.

g. A volunteer reads the affirmation aloud at the bottom left of the page.

h. Teens compose their own affirmation with its accompanying action; share aloud.

i. Teens cut out the affirmations and post them in prominent places (wallet, mirror, computer, *My Affirmations and More* display, etc.).

Enrichment Activities

a. Write the following on the board:

"Helpful strategies that didn't work in one situation, but did or could work in other situations."
> *Example: I was honest, open, and direct in an assertive way with someone.*
> *It didn't work very well, though it can work in another situation.*

b. Teens share their own examples.

ENTHUSIASM 5

Protect your enthusiasm from the negativity and fear of others.
Never decide to do nothing because you can only do little.
Do what you can.
You would be surprised what "little" acts have done for our world.

~ Steve Maraboli

Take-Away Skills

Conditions and Behavior (1), *Frequency and Duration* (2), and/or *Accomplishment* (3) **statements for each activity may be used in educational and/or treatment planning, and also used to measure progress toward goals. These Take-Away skills promote real life outcomes and behavioral changes.**

EXAMPLES

1. *Conditions and Behavior* – **a skill or healthy habit to replace a previous less effective behavior or habit.**
   - Now, I … *(less effective or undesired behavior).*
   - When I … *(when do I do this?),*
     instead I will … *(more effective or desired new behavior)* in _____ out of _____ opportunities.
2. **Frequency and Duration – a skill or healthy habit not necessarily tied to a condition or previous behavior.**
   - I will *(describe the behavior)* _____ times per _____.
3. **Accomplishment – an outcome that is a one-time accomplishment.**
   - I will *(describe the accomplishment)* by _____ *(date).*

CHAPTER 5 - Enthusiasm
Take-Away Skills Examples

GO WITH FLOW – PASS THE PAGE

Flow is a mental state of operation in which a person performing
an activity is fully immersed in a feeling of energized focus,
full involvement, and enjoyment of the process of the activity.

Each player anonymously adds a response to one of the questions:

What makes video games fascinating?

1. _____
2. _____
3. _____
4. _____
5. _____
6. _____
7. _____
8. _____
9. _____
10. _____

What other activities do people find fascinating or enjoyable?

1. _____
2. _____
3. _____
4. _____
5. _____
6. _____
7. _____
8. _____
9. _____
10. _____

GO WITH FLOW – IMMERSE YOURSELF

Flow is a mental state of operation in which a person performing
an activity is fully immersed in a feeling of energized focus,
full involvement, and enjoyment of the process of the activity.

**Show yourself totally absorbed in a productive activity you enjoy.
Show what's in your heart, head, and your surroundings.**

GO WITH FLOW – WHAT'S MINE?

Flow is a mental state of operation in which a person performing
an activity is fully immersed in a feeling of energized focus,
full involvement, and enjoyment of the process of the activity.

Think about one productive activity you like that meets all these "flow" conditions.

I become fully focused.
I am energized.
I lose my sense of time.
I forget myself.
I feel challenged.
My skills match the challenge.
Just doing this matters more than the results.
I feel a satisfying sense of well-being.

Respond in the thought bubble.

I go with flow when I am …

AFFIRMATIONS

Example:	My Own Affirmation …	My Action …
I immerse myself in productive activity.		

GO WITH FLOW
FOR THE FACILITATOR

I. Purpose
To find one's state of flow: Total immersion in an activity, energized, and enjoying the process.
To find productive flow: creating, learning, helping, working, collaborating, advocating, etc.

II. Skills
Identify ten aspects of video games that illustrate "go with flow":
Active (not passive like watching TV); complete concentration; high motivation; clear goals; immediate feedback; enjoyment of the process; learning opportunities; loss of sense of time; little attention to physical needs e.g. eating, sleeping; a balance between skills and task demands; etc.
Identify ten other productive activities that may be equally engrossing.
Depict and/or describe self totally immersed in a productive activity.
State what one is doing when eight conditions of "go with flow" are met.
Compose an affirmation with its accompanying action.
Identify three examples of group "go with flow."

III. Possible Activities
a. Distribute one photocopy of the *Go with Flow – Pass the Page* handout, page 75. A volunteer reads the definition of "Go with Flow" aloud. Allow time for discussion or clarification.
Teens pass the page, add ideas, and then volunteers read responses aloud.
b. Distribute the *Go with Flow – Immerse Yourself* handout, page, 76. A volunteer reads the information and directions aloud.
Elicit examples of productive activity:
Participation in sports, art, choir, band, orchestra, dance, math, writing, theater, nature, work, volunteering, advocacy, spirituality, etc.
Teens use drawings, icons, words, etc. to show their thoughts, feelings, and surroundings.
Teens share their responses, and receive peer feedback.
c. Distribute the *Go with Flow –What's Mine?* handout, page 77. Volunteers read the information and directions aloud.
Teens complete their thought bubbles, share responses, and receive peer feedback.
d. A volunteer reads the affirmation aloud at the bottom left of the page.
e. Teens compose their own affirmation with its accompanying action; share aloud.
f. Teens cut out the affirmations and post them in prominent places (wallet, mirror, computer, *My Affirmations and More* display, etc.).

IV. Enrichment Activities
Teens discuss experiences with "group flow."
Possibilities
• Members of a club coordinating activities
• Teamwork toward a goal in sports or band or chorus, etc.
• Social cohesion as group members support each other
• Volunteer in a soup kitchen, fund raiser for a charity or team trip, etc.

The Real Zeal – Descriptions

ZEAL = motivation, energy, and enthusiasm for a goal or a cause.

This quotation describes the meaning of the word ZEAL very well …

Live your truth.

Express your love.

Share your enthusiasm.

Take action towards your dreams.

Walk your talk.

Dance and sing to your music.

Embrace your blessings.

Make today worth remembering.

~ Steve Maraboli

Diagram the quotation above with the following icons …

 Draw a star in front of a line that has meaning to you.

 Draw a thumbs up sign in front of a line you agree with but don't always do.

 Draw a smiley face in front of a line that is easy for you to do.

 Put a question mark in front of a line you are unsure about.

 Draw a frowny face in front of a line that is difficult for you to do.

 Draw a wishbone in front of a line you would like to know how to do.

The Real Zeal – Truth

ZEAL = motivation, energy, and enthusiasm for a goal or a cause.

You demonstrate zeal when you "live your truth."

My Truth Journal

I believe …

_____

_____

_____

_____

I can "live (my) truth" by …

_____

_____

_____

_____

To "Walk (my) talk" means …

_____

_____

_____

_____

Ways to "dance and sing" to my own "music" are …

_____

_____

_____

_____

The Real Zeal – Appreciation

ZEAL = motivation, energy, and enthusiasm for a goal or a cause.

You demonstrate zeal when you express your appreciation.

Surprise people you care about.
Compose a message on each note below.
Cut out the notes and place them on people's computers, mirrors, etc.

The Real Zeal - Share

ZEAL = motivation, energy, and enthusiasm for a goal or a cause.

**You demonstrate zeal when you "share your enthusiasm."
Share your zeal for your goal or cause by decorating a door.**

Plan your door decoration below.

**"Take action towards your dreams" by decorating a door at home or
school (with permission).**

The Real Zeal – Blessings

ZEAL = motivation, energy, and enthusiasm for a goal or a cause.

What do you have to be grateful for?

My Blessings List

AFFIRMATIONS

Example:	My Own Affirmation ...	My Action ...
Enthusiasm is my new habit.		

The Real Zeal
FOR THE FACILITATOR

I. Purpose
To develop zeal for life.

II. Skills
Define zeal.
Demonstrate eight aspects of zeal.
Compose an affirmation with its accompanying action.

III. Possible Activities
Plan to present the series of sessions over several days or as a *Real Zeal Day* workshop.
a. Distribute *The Real Zeal – Descriptions*, page 79.
   Volunteers read definition, quotation, and directions aloud.
   Teens complete the page, share their responses and receive peer feedback.
b. Distribute *The Real Zeal – Truth*, page 80.
   Discuss the difference between literal (exact) and figurative (symbolic) meanings.
   Example: "Dance and sing to your music" could suggest "Enjoy pursuing your passion."
   Teens complete the page, share their responses, and receive peer feedback.
c. Distribute *The Real Zeal – Appreciation*, page 81.
   A volunteer reads the directions aloud.
   Teens complete the page, share their responses, and receive peer feedback.
d. Distribute *The Real Zeal – Share*, page 82.
   A volunteer reads the directions aloud.
   Encourage teens to use images and words for their door decoration plans.
   Teens complete the page, share their sketches and ideas, and receive peer feedback.
e. Distribute *The Real Zeal – Blessings*, page 83.
   Teens complete the *My Blessing Lists*, share their responses, and receive peer feedback.
f. A volunteer reads the affirmation aloud at the bottom left of the page.
g. Teens compose their own affirmation with its accompanying action; share aloud.
h. Teens cut out the affirmations and post them in prominent places (wallet, mirror, computer, *My Affirmations and More* display, etc.).

IV. Enrichment Activities
Teens start a *The Real Zeal* door decoration trend.
• Teams take turns decorating the door in the room each week or month.
• Team members focus on common goals and causes, or motivational themes.

Dance in the Rain

Life isn't about waiting for the storm to pass ...
It's about learning to dance in the rain.

~ Vivian Greene

What often happens to people who wait to pursue
their dreams until all conditions are absolutely perfect?

**Create a cartoon strip portraying you joyfully doing whatever you need to do now,
to achieve your dream, despite conditions that could delay or stop you.**

AFFIRMATIONS

Example:	My Own Affirmation ...	My Action ...
I pursue my dreams.		

Dance in the Rain
FOR THE FACILITATOR

I. Purpose
To maintain enthusiasm despite less than perfect conditions.

II. Skills
Interpret a quotation.
Show actions toward a dream despite situations that could delay, deter, or distract.
Compose an affirmation with its accompanying action.
Portray actions toward a goal through pantomime.
Interpret others' pantomimed actions toward goals.

III. Possible Activities
a. Distribute the *Dance in the Rain* handout.
b. A volunteer reads the quotation aloud.
c. Teens share their interpretations.
d. A volunteer reads the question and elicits responses.
   Example: People may never pursue their dreams because conditions are hardly ever perfect.
e. Teens complete the activity, share their cartoon strips, and receive peer feedback.
f. A volunteer reads the affirmation aloud at the bottom left of the page.
g. Teens compose their own affirmation with its accompanying action; share aloud.
h. Teens cut out the affirmations and post them in prominent places (wallet, mirror, computer, *My Affirmations & More* display, etc.).

IV. Enrichment Activities
a. Teens compose dances or pantomimes to express their enthusiasm for their goals. Teens may enlist peers to act as people who try to prevent or promote the pursuit of their goals.
b. Peers guess the message being portrayed.

Recharge

Have you noticed that the electric socket that recharges your cell phone looks like a face?

What does your power source look like?
(POWER SOURCE = something or someone who motivates, energizes, or inspires you)

You may create the image with your eyes open. Or … try closing your eyes.
Let your imagination guide your hand. When you are finished, explain the image.

AFFIRMATIONS

Example:	My Own Affirmation …	My Action …
I renew my inner self.		

Recharge
FOR THE FACILITATOR

I. Purpose
To tap into a personal power source.

II. Skills
Acknowledge the need to recharge emotionally, spiritually, etc.
Draw an image of one's power source visually, or using imagination and the tactile sense.
Interpret the image.
Compose an affirmation with its accompanying action.
Identify ways to recharge physically, emotionally, spiritually, intellectually, and socially.

III. Possible Activities
a. Distribute the *Recharge* handout.
b. A volunteer reads the information and directions aloud.
c. Teens complete their images, share their responses, and receive peer feedback.
   Possibilities
   - A person
   - Creative expression
   - Inspirational literature
   - Meditation
   - One's center, core, inner strength
   - Places or objects in nature
   - Places where teens pursue their passions
   - Spiritual or religious figures or symbols
d. A volunteer reads the affirmation aloud at the bottom left of the page.
e. Teens compose their own affirmation with its accompanying action; share aloud.
f. Teens cut out the affirmations and post them in prominent places (wallet, mirror, computer, *My Affirmations and More* display, etc.).

IV. Enrichment Activities
Teens discuss ways to recharge in various ways:
- Emotionally – share feelings with understanding, helpful people, etc.
- Intellectually – read, brain games, discussion, debate, etc.
- Physically – exercise, adequate sleep, nutrition, etc.
- Socially – friends, family, clubs, work, volunteering, etc.
- Spiritually – worship, songs of praise, youth group, etc.

SELF-DETERMINATION 6

*You cannot change your destination overnight,
But you can change your direction overnight.*

~ Jim Rohn

Take-Away Skills

Conditions and Behavior (1), *Frequency and Duration* (2), and/or *Accomplishment* (3) statements for each activity may be used in educational and/or treatment planning, and also used to measure progress toward goals. These Take-Away skills promote real life outcomes and behavioral changes.

EXAMPLES

1. *Conditions and Behavior* – a skill or healthy habit to replace a previous less effective behavior or habit.
   - Now, I … *(less effective or undesired behavior).*
   - When I … *(when do I do this?),*
     instead I will … *(more effective or desired new behavior)* in _____ out of _____ opportunities.
2. **Frequency and Duration** – a skill or healthy habit not necessarily tied to a condition or previous behavior.
   - I will *(describe the behavior)* _____ times per _____.
3. **Accomplishment** – an outcome that is a one-time accomplishment.
   - I will *(describe the accomplishment)* by _____ *(date).*

CHAPTER 6 - Self-Determination
Take-Away Skills Examples

Accomplishment
- *I will make an appointment with my school counselor to meet by Monday.*

Frequency and Duration
- *I will discuss my issues honestly with my counselor for 30 minutes once weekly for the next 4 weeks.*

Conditions and Behavior
- Now, I … *use a drug or alcohol for comfort.*
- When I … *feel upset,*
  instead I will … *discuss coping skills with my counselor, in 5 out of 5 opportunities.*

Conditions and Behavior
- Now, I … *copy someone's homework.*
- When I … *feel clueless about an assignment,*
  instead I will … *ask the teacher to help me understand in 5 out of 5 opportunities.*

Accomplishment
- *I will raise my GPA, without cheating, by the next semester.*

CHAPTER 6 - Self-Determination
Take-Away Skills Examples

Emotional Self-Protection

**A movie based on a true story showed a boy born with a deficient immune system.
He had to spend his life in a completely sterile environment – a plastic bubble.
Just as the boy was protected physically, we can all protect ourselves emotionally.**

1. Draw yourself as a stick figure in the bubble below.
2. Inside the bubble, show your protective thoughts, feelings, and actions.
3. Outside the bubble, show the thoughts, feelings, and actions that could harm you.
4. Highlight the arrows pointing away from your bubble to show that …

You can protect yourself and preserve your emotional well-being.

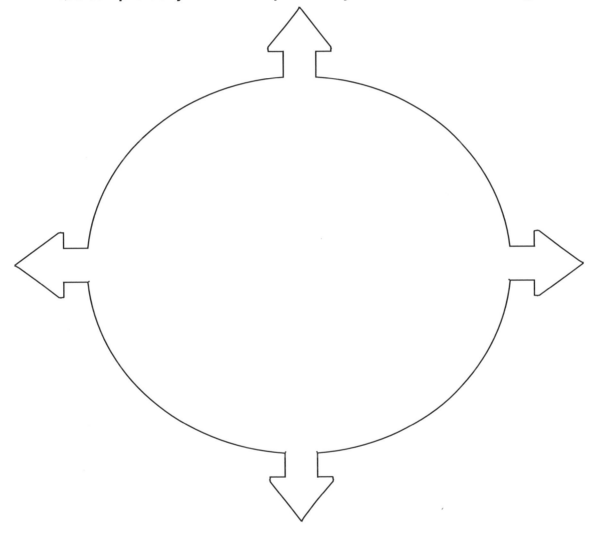

AFFIRMATIONS

Example:	My Own Affirmation …	My Action …
I protect my emotional well-being.		

Emotional Self-Protection
FOR THE FACILITATOR

Purpose
To recognize and use the self-protective power of positive thoughts, feelings, and actions.

Skills
Identify protective, positive thoughts, feelings, and actions.
Identify harmful, negative thoughts, feelings, and actions.
Depict emotional self-protection as an impenetrable bubble of positive thoughts, feelings, and actions.
Compose an affirmation with its accompanying action.
Brainstorm symptoms and situations that require outside intervention.

Possible Activities
a. Distribute the *Emotional Self-Protection* handout.
b. Volunteers read the information and directions aloud.
c. Teens use sketches and/or words to complete the activity.
d. Teens share their responses and receive peer feedback.
e. A volunteer reads the affirmation aloud at the bottom left of the page.
f. Teens compose their own affirmation with its accompanying action; share aloud.
g. Teens cut out the affirmations and post them in prominent places (wallet, mirror, computer, *My Affirmations and More* display, etc.).

Enrichment Activities
a. Teens brainstorm responses to the following question:
"When do you need more protection than your positive bubble?"
   Possibilities:
   - If being bullied
   - If being abused
   - If feeling fear, anger, depression, etc., and those feelings do not go away despite positive self-protection
   - If addiction is experienced
   - If wanting to harm self/others
   - If experiencing a situation that requires conflict resolution with other people
   - If confused about an issue

b. Teens identify helpful resources:
   Possibilities:
   - Trusted adult family members
   - Counselors, teachers, youth group advisors
   - Mental health and addiction recovery professionals

Go for It! Take Action

Find one word of two or more letters below, in one minute.

I R U V Z J

How would you feel about finding another word just like that?
a. Capable and powerful.
b. Clueless and powerless.

Now, find a word in these letters

E O P W R

People who try their best, but can't solve a problem (like finding a word that isn't there) may feel powerless.
Then, when they COULD solve a problem, they may think they CAN'T.

Create a scenario with a person who acted powerless, yet had the power to take action.

Once upon a time, a person named _____ acted powerless by

_____

_____

_____

_____

_____

_____

This person really had the power to take action by _____

_____

_____

_____

_____

_____

_____

AFFIRMATIONS

Example:	My Own Affirmation …	My Action …
I have power over my actions.		

Go for It! Meet Your Needs

Hungry Monkeys

Zookeepers met all the monkeys' needs.
The monkeys were given food every day for years.

Then, the monkeys were suddenly released into the jungle.
Food was abundant.
The monkeys had to find it.

How do you think the monkeys reacted?

a. *They searched for food.*
b. *They waited for someone to feed them.*

The monkeys did not search for food. At the zoo, they learned they would be fed.
Then, when they needed to search for food on their own, they thought they couldn't.
The monkeys learned to expect others to meet all their needs.

Some people also expect others to meet their needs.
*When everything is done for people, they tend to think they can't do anything
for themselves.*
Then, when they need to meet their own needs, they think they can't.

Try writing a couplet about meeting your own needs.
A couplet has two lines that may or may not rhyme.
Each line has the same number of syllables.
Example Title: My Mood
Must people make me happy?
Or is my mood up to me?

Title _____

_____

_____

AFFIRMATIONS

Example:	My Own Affirmation …	My Action …
I do what I can for myself.		

Go for It! Act Powerful

People who realize they have personal power can act on it.

Write the letter for the corresponding powerful action in front of each powerless statement.

PowerLESS Statements	PowerFUL Actions
_____ Others caused my problem.	A. I make a decision today.
_____ No one ever talks to me.	B. I will risk rejection to find acceptance.
_____ I just can't do math.	C. I start with a math problem I can solve.
_____ I'm out of shape because I have no trainer.	D. I see factors that were part of the situation.
_____ I'm sad because of issues in my past.	E. I take a step to solve my problem.
_____ I'm stuck in an abusive situation.	F. I seek out like-minded friends.
_____ It's all my fault.	G. I revise my schedule.
_____ I can't make my own decisions.	H. I learn from my past.
_____ My schedule is too busy.	I. I exercise regularly no matter what.
_____ I can't make friends.	J. I start a conversation today.
_____ I'll never ask anyone out after rejections.	K. I tell a trusted adult about the abuse.
My own powerLESS statement …	_My own powerFUL action …_
_____	_____
_____	_____
_____	_____
_____	_____

AFFIRMATIONS

Example:	My Own Affirmation …	My Action …
If I seem stuck, I get unstuck.		

Go for It
FOR THE FACILITATOR

I. Purpose
To prevent powerlessness by taking positive actions.

II. Skills
Describe a person acting powerless in a situation.
Note action(s) the person could have taken.
Create a couplet about meeting one's personal needs rather than unnecessary reliance on others.
Substitute twelve powerful actions for corresponding powerless statements.
Compose three affirmations with corresponding actions.
Identify healthy risks one wants to take.

III. Possible Activities
Present the *Go for It!* handouts separately, and in order, during the same or subsequent sessions.
  a. Distribute *Go for It! – Take Action,* page 95.
- Tell teens to find one word with two or more letters in one minute.
  (Teens do **not** yet know that there are no words in this set of letters).
- Call "Time's Up!" after one minute.
- Teens decide how they feel, (a. or b.)
- Teens find the word "power."
- Teens read the text, and discuss the tendency to act powerless when problems seem unsolvable.
- Teens create and share their scenarios, and receive peer feedback.
- A volunteer reads the affirmation aloud at the bottom left of the page.
- Teens compose their own affirmation with its accompanying action; share aloud.
- Teens cut out the affirmations and post them in prominent places (wallet, mirror, computer, *My Affirmations and More* display, etc.).

  b. Distribute *Go for It! Meet Your Needs,* page 96.
- Volunteers read the information aloud.
- Teens create and share their couplets and receive peer feedback.
- Teens proceed with affirmations as described in "a."

  c. Distribute *Go for It! Act Powerful,* page 97.
- A volunteer reads the information aloud.
- Teens complete the matching exercise and review their responses.
  Answer key
  E, J, C, I, H, K, D, A, G, F, B, plus individually composed statements and actions.
- Teens proceed with affirmations as described under "a."

IV. Enrichment Activities
  a. Teens review the meaning of "Go for it!"
(To give it a try, or do what you need to do).
  b. Teens discuss the meaning of "Go out on a limb."
(To express an opinion not shared by others, or put self in a difficult, awkward, or vulnerable position).
  c. Teens share ways they would like to go out on a limb
(Healthy risks they want to take).

UN-Powered or EM-Powered?

When UN-powered, you give power and authority to others.
When EM-powered, you give power and authority to yourself.
Empowered people are strong and confident in controlling their lives by claiming their rights.

Add three un-powered examples in the left-hand column. Leave the right-hand column blank.

UN-Powered	EM-Powered
Ex: You fail a final and have to re-take the class. *Ex: You are abused by a partner and do nothing.* #1 #2 #3	*You ask for help when you know you're struggling.* *You break up and report the abuse.* #1 #2 #3

AFFIRMATIONS

Example:	My Own Affirmation …	My Action …
I am empowered!		

Un-Powered or Em-Powered?
FOR THE FACILITATOR

I. Purpose
To empower self to promote favorable outcomes.

II. Skills
Identify three un-powered examples.
Describe three or more em-powered actions.
Compose an affirmation with its accompanying action.
Personalize a quotation about problem prevention.

III. Possible Activities
a. Distribute the *Un-Powered or Em-Powered?* handout.
b. Volunteers read the information and examples aloud.
c. Teens write their un-powered examples.
d. Select the preferred format from the following:
   Pass the Page
   - Teens pass the page and peers each add one em-powered action to each page.
   - Teens retrieve their own pages, read both columns aloud, and receive peer feedback.
   Peers Lead Discussions
   - Teens take turns reading one of their un-powered situations aloud.
   - Peers discuss possible em-powered actions.
   - Teens repeat the process with their second and third examples as time permits.
e. A volunteer reads the affirmation aloud at the bottom left of the page.
f. Teens compose their own affirmation with its accompanying action; share aloud.
g. Teens cut out the affirmations and post them in prominent places (wallet, mirror, computer, *My Affirmations and More* display, etc.).

IV. Enrichment Activities
a. Write the Benjamin Franklin quotation on the board:
   "An ounce of prevention is worth a pound of cure."
b. Teens interpret its meaning.
c. Teens share personal stories of times they did or did not prevent an unfavorable outcome.

100

MY CIRCLE OF CONTROL

The goal is to spend time and energy on issues in our life that are within our control. Worrying and trying to solve issues outside of our control is a waste of time and energy.

In the middle circle, write the issues that are within your control.

In the outside circle, write the issues that are outside of your control.

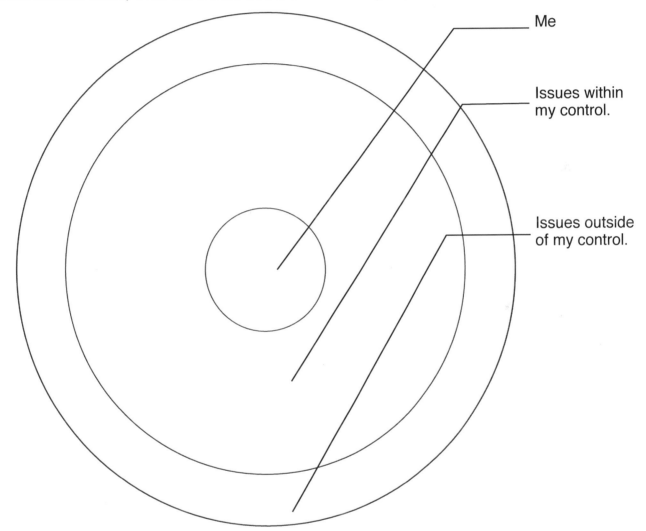

Me

Issues within my control.

Issues outside of my control.

Now, highlight the issues that are WITHIN YOUR CONTROL

AFFIRMATIONS

Example:	My Own Affirmation …	My Action …
I focus on issues within my control.		

MY CIRCLE OF CONTROL
FOR THE FACILITATOR

I. Purpose
To focus time and energy on issues within personal control.

II. Skills
Identify issues within personal control.
Visually focus by highlighting them.
Identify issues outside personal control.
Compose an affirmation with its accompanying action.
Describe one's primary focus for the current week.

III. Possible Activities
a. Distribute the *My Circle of Control* handout.
b. Volunteers read the information and directions aloud.
c. Teens complete their diagrams, share responses, and receive peer feedback.
   Possibilities
   Issues within my control – my thoughts, feelings, actions, values, habits; how I
      treat people, etc.
   Issues outside my control – other people's thoughts, feelings, actions; the past;
      aspects of the future.
d. A volunteer reads the affirmation aloud at the bottom left of the page.
e. Teens compose their own affirmation with its accompanying action; share aloud.
f. Teens cut out the affirmations and post them in prominent places (wallet, mirror, computer,
   My Affirmations and More display, etc.)

IV. Enrichment Activities
a. Teens turn over their handouts.
b. Teens title the page "My First Focus."
c. Teens specify the most important aspect of their lives to focus on during the current week.
d. Teens need to be specific.
   Examples
   "My thoughts about …" (rather than just "My thoughts.")
   "My actions toward … will be to …" (rather than just "My actions.")
e. Teens share their responses and receive peer feedback.

DECISION-MAKING POWER

Self-determination is the power to make your own decisions.

Keeping in mind decisions you need to make or have already made, select two of the sentence starters below that have meaning to you. Then journal your thoughts on the back of this page.

1. A current situation that warns me to stop and think is …
2. The pros and cons of my current decision are …
3. Although the decision is mine, it might help to talk with …
4. Some sources of information about this decision are …
5. A great past decision of mine was …
6. A past decision made without thinking was …
7. A past decision taught me …
8. I wish I had made a different decision about …
9. A person I allow to influence my decisions too much is …
10. A time I decided not to decide was …
11. A decision based on what I wanted at the moment was …
12. A decision based on a goal was …
13. I may seek spiritual guidance about …
14. A decision that needs more thought is …
15. If I let my fears rule, I will decide to …
16. If I let my hope rule, I will decide to …
17. If I let people decide for me, I will …
18. I have decided to find a way to …
19. I have decided to control my own response in this situation …
20. A decision based on my goal, rather than what I want now, is …
21. I plan to talk to my parents/caregivers about my decision to …
22. A decision I plan to share with my partner is …
23. I plan to tell my best friend about my decision to …
24. A decision I will discuss with a trusted adult is …
25. A decision based on my values is to …

AFFIRMATIONS

Example:	My Own Affirmation …	My Action …
I make informed decisions.		

DECISION-MAKING POWER
FOR THE FACILITATOR

I. Purpose
To recognize decision-making rights, responsibilities, and considerations.

II. Skills
Identify the link between self-determination and decisions.
Document personal application of two or more decision-making concepts.
Compose an affirmation with its accompanying action.
Graphically depict the portion of one's life that reflects personal decisions.

III. Possible Activities
a. Distribute the *Decision-Making Power* handout.
b. Volunteers read the information, directions, and sentence-starters aloud.
c. Teens journal their thoughts.
d. Volunteers share their responses and receive peer feedback.
   Suggestions:
   - Consider presenting the page during subsequent sessions.
     Each time, teens choose different sentences to complete.
   - Consider a Twenty-Five Day Challenge.
     Teens complete one sentence per day, and save entries in a journal, or on their phones or computer.
     After twenty-five days, volunteers share their most meaningful entries.
e. A volunteer reads the affirmation aloud at the bottom left of the page.
f. Teens compose their own affirmation with its accompanying action; share aloud.
g. Teens cut out the affirmations and post them in prominent places (wallet, mirror, computer, *My Affirmations and More* display, etc.).

IV. Enrichment Activity
a. Teens turn over their handouts.
b. Teens draw a big circle.
c. Teens title the circle "My Life."
d. Teens shade in the portion of the circle (their life) that reflects decisions they have made.
e. Teens share and explain their responses, and receive peer feedback.

THE GREATEST GIFT

I believe the greatest gift I can conceive
of having from anyone is
to be seen by them, heard by them,
to be understood and touched by them.

~ Virginia Satir

Sometimes we perceive that asking for, or receiving help, is a weakness.
Accepting help means we are social beings who need each other from time to time.

I can let _____ see the real me by

_____

_____

_____

_____

I can let _____ help me by

_____

_____

_____

_____

To be heard and understood, I can express my needs by saying _____

_____

_____

_____

_____

_____

AFFIRMATIONS

Example:	My Own Affirmation …	My Action …
I admit my human need for help.		

THE GREATEST GIFT
FOR THE FACILITATOR

I. Purpose
To recognize that self-determination has limits. It involves knowing when to ask for and accept help.
To acknowledge accepting help as part of being human.

II. Skills
Share truths about self.
State needs.
Identify ways others can help.
Compose an affirmation and its accompanying action.
Identify others' needs and ways to help.

III. Possible Activities
a. Distribute *The Greatest Gift* handout.
b. A volunteer reads the quotation aloud and encourages reactions.
c. Teens complete the sentence starters, share their responses, and receive peer feedback.
d. A volunteer reads the affirmation aloud at the bottom left of the page.
e. Teens compose their own affirmation with its accompanying action; share aloud.
f. Teens cut out the affirmations and post them in prominent places (wallet, mirror, computer, *My Affirmations and More* display, etc.).

IV. Enrichment Activities
a. Write on the board the rest of the Virginia Satir quotation:
   "The greatest gift I can give is to see, hear, understand and to touch another person."
b. Teens identify ways to do the following:
   - See, rather than look away.
   - Hear, rather than shut out.
   - Understand, rather than judge.
   - Touch others' lives.
c. Teens share ways they have helped others in the past.
d. Teens share ways they have been helped in the past.
e. Teens discuss situations in which they have helped others but not themselves.

POSITIVE ACTIONS (7)

> *You've always had the power my dear,*
> *You just had to learn it for yourself.*
> ~ The Wizard of Oz

Take-Away Skills

Conditions and Behavior (1), *Frequency and Duration* (2), and/or *Accomplishment* (3) statements for each activity may be used in educational and/or treatment planning, and also used to measure progress toward goals. These Take-Away skills promote real life outcomes and behavioral changes.

EXAMPLES

1. *Conditions and Behavior* – a skill or healthy habit to replace a previous less effective behavior or habit.
   - Now, I … *(less effective or undesired behavior).*
   - When I … *(when do I do this?),*
     instead I will … *(more effective or desired new behavior)* in _____ out of _____ opportunities.
2. **Frequency and Duration** – a skill or healthy habit not necessarily tied to a condition or previous behavior.
   - I will *(describe the behavior)* _____ times per _____.
3. **Accomplishment** – an outcome that is a one-time accomplishment.
   - I will *(describe the accomplishment)* by _____ *(date).*

CHAPTER 7 - Positive Actions
Take-Away Skills Examples

CHAPTER 7 - Positive Actions
Take-Away Skills Examples

109

Pay It Forward

Pay it forward = receive kindness and repay by being kind to someone else.

In the arrow below, note how someone was kind to you. Describe how you can pay it forward.

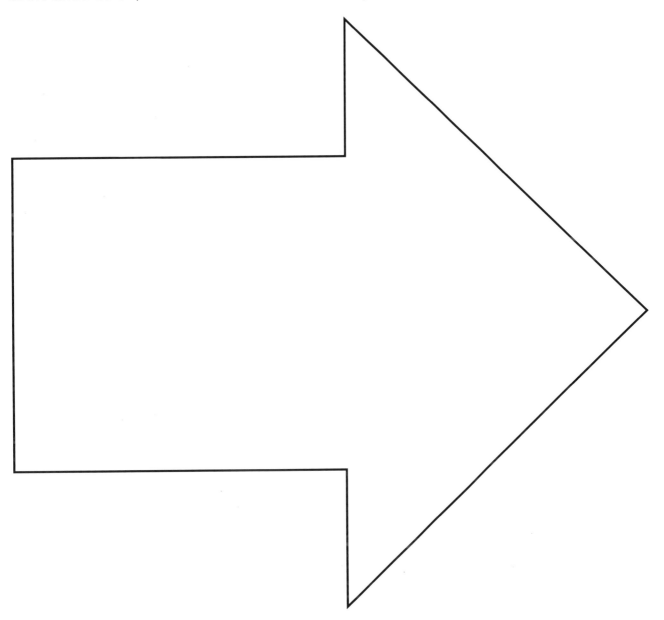

AFFIRMATIONS

Example:	My Own Affirmation …	My Action …
I recognize and repay kindness.		

Pay It Forward
FOR THE FACILITATOR

I. Purpose
To perform acts of kindness after being the beneficiary of kindness.

II. Skills
Interpret the meaning of "Pay it forward."
Identify a kindness shown to self.
Describe how to show similar kindness toward another person.
Compose an affirmation with its accompanying action.
Describe a plan to "Teach it forward."

III. Possible Activities
a. Distribute the *Pay It Forward* handout.
b. A volunteer reads the information and directions aloud.
Tell teens "Although we do act kindly toward people who are kind to us, for this activity we will repay the kindness to someone *other than* the person who was kind to us."
c. Teens write in their arrows, share their responses, and receive peer feedback.
d. Teens are encouraged to carry out their plans within the next week, and then share how they felt after paying forward the kindness.
e. Teens may wish to explore the novel and/or the movie, *Pay It Forward*, by Catherine Ryan Hyde.
f. A volunteer reads the affirmation aloud at the bottom left of the page.
g. Teens compose their own affirmation with its accompanying action; share aloud.
h. Teens cut out the affirmations and post them in prominent places (wallet, mirror, computer, *My Affirmations and More* display, etc.).

IV. Enrichment Activities
a. Teens repeat the activity with the *Teach It Forward* theme.
b. Teens teach a concept in class, help a peer with homework, teach someone to play an instrument, etc.

Intentional Kindness – Benevolence

Benevolence = an act of kindness

List at least ten acts of intentional kindness.

1. _____
2. _____
3. _____
4. _____
5. _____
6. _____
7. _____
8. _____
9. _____
10. _____
11. _____
12. _____
13. _____
14. _____
15. _____
16. _____
17. _____
18. _____

AFFIRMATIONS

Example:	My Own Affirmation …	My Action …
I think about others' needs.		

Intentional Kindness – Whodunit?

In a Whodunit mystery, you don't know who did it *(the crime)* until the end.
In this Whodunit activity,
people may never know who did it *(the act of kindness)*. And that's OK!

Examples:

Make My Day
    Create greeting cards with uplifting art and messages.
    Tell a store manager about an exceptional employee.

Shopping Spree
    If you decide not to buy an item, replace it to the proper location.
    Pick up litter from the parking lot.

Dine Kindly
    Return a tray someone left on the table.
    Provide positive online reviews for great food and service.

Anonymous acts of kindness I will do are ...

_____

_____

_____

_____

_____

_____

_____

_____

_____

_____

_____

AFFIRMATIONS

Example:	My Own Affirmation ...	My Action ...
Secret kindness gives me secret pleasure.		

Intentional Self-Kindness – Weekly Journal

**Think about adopting an intentional kindness habit for yourself.
Keep a confidential record of your weekly acts of kindness to YOU.
Create corresponding self-affirmations.**

Date	My Intentional Act of Kindness	Self-Affirmation
Sunday, May 7	*I made myself a good breakfast before going to school to take the final.*	*I prepare physically and mentally for exams.*
Sunday		
Monday		
Tuesday		
Wednesday		
Thursday		
Friday		
Saturday		

Intentional Kindness - Weekly Journal

FOR THE FACILITATOR

I. Purpose
To perform intentional acts of kindness.

II. Skills
Identify ten or more acts of kindness.
Describe two or more planned, anonymous, acts of kindness.
Record acts of kindness with their accompanying self-affirmations.
Exchange items, and help, during a Swap Meet.
Compose an affirmation with its accompanying action.

III. Possible Activities
Present the *Intentional Kindness* handouts separately, during the same or subsequent sessions.
  a. Distribute *Intentional Kindness – Benevolence*, page 113.
  - A volunteer reads the information and directions aloud.
  - Teens complete their lists.
  - Volunteers participate in the following Benevolence Bee:
  Teens stand and take turns sharing one act of kindness from their lists or name one they just thought of for each round.
  A volunteer lists the acts of kindness on board.
  Teens continue taking turns to share one act of kindness not previously listed.
  When a teen states a duplicate act of kindness, or does not share a new idea, the person sits.
  The last teen(s) standing gets applause.
  - A volunteer reads the affirmation aloud at the bottom left of the page.
  - Teens compose their own affirmation with its accompanying action; share aloud.
  - Teens cut out the affirmations and post them in prominent places (wallet, mirror, computer,
  - *My Affirmations and More* display, etc.).

  b. Distribute *Intentional Kindness – Whodunit?* page 114.
  - Volunteers read the information and examples aloud.
  - Teens complete "Places I go …" and "Anonymous acts of kindness …"
  - Teens share responses, and receive peer feedback.
  - Teens proceed with affirmations as described under "a."
  c. Distribute *Intentional Kindness – Weekly Journal*, page 115.
  - A volunteer reads the directions aloud.
  - Teens discuss the personal benefits of kindness to self.
  - Teens add to the journal daily.

IV. Enrichment Activities
Teens plan a Swap Meet.
  - Teens provide anonymous lists of what they need.
  - Teens provide anonymous lists of what they have to donate.
  - Teens look over the lists to determine what to donate and/or take.
  Items may be tangible, e.g., a back pack.
  Items may be intangible, e.g., help with homework.
  - On Swap Meet Day, people anonymously bring and take tangible items.
  - Teens who can help with intangible items (homework, etc.), meet to discuss arrangements.

Creative Resilience

> **Resilience is rebounding after a disappointment.**
>
> **Creativity is using the imagination to produce an object or experience.**

Creatively expressing feelings helps build resilience.
Feelings about a disappointment can be expressed in many ways.
Check those items that look appealing to you. Add any others that might apply.

- ☐ Act
- ☐ Art
- ☐ Back stage theater
- ☐ Bake
- ☐ Band
- ☐ Choir
- ☐ Choreography
- ☐ Cooking
- ☐ Crafts
- ☐ Create a special meal
- ☐ Dance
- ☐ Doodle
- ☐ Draw
- ☐ Event plans
- ☐ Floral arrangements
- ☐ Garden

- ☐ Landscape
- ☐ Lyrics
- ☐ Magazine collage
- ☐ Orchestra
- ☐ Paint
- ☐ Photography
- ☐ Play instrument
- ☐ Poetry
- ☐ Puzzles
- ☐ Sculpture
- ☐ Sing
- ☐ Stories
- ☐ Videography
- ☐ Other _____
- ☐ Other _____
- ☐ Other _____

On the back of this page share your ideas by writing or sketching how you can be creative, to help you rebound from a disappointment.

(Your work is private. You may share if you wish.)

AFFIRMATIONS

Example:	My Own Affirmation …	My Action …
I use my creativity to express my feelings.		

Creative Resilience
FOR THE FACILITATOR

I. Purpose
To help build resilience through creativity.

II. Skills
Define resilience and creativity. State the link between them.
Creatively express feelings about recent or current disappointment.
Compose an affirmation with its accompanying action.
Research and report about creative people who address disappointments through their work.

III. Possible Activities
a. Distribute the *Creative Resilience* handout.
b. Volunteers read the information and directions aloud.
c. Teens complete their creative expressions on the back of the handout.
d. Volunteers share their responses.
e. Peers do not provide feedback about the creations.
f. A volunteer reads the affirmation aloud at the bottom left of the page.
g. Teens compose their own affirmation with its accompanying action; share aloud.
h. Teens cut out the affirmations and post them in prominent places (wallet, mirror, computer, *My Affirmations and More* display, etc.).
i. If time permits, or during the next session, teens may further develop their creations. Possibilities:
   - Add paint to sketches or use clay to sculpt.
   - Perform dances, songs, or plays.
   - Present musical compositions or lyrics.
   - Read stories or poems aloud.
   - Submit the work for publication in the school newspaper.
   - Display work on a bulletin board in school.

IV. Enrichment Activities
a. Teens research and report about artists, writers, composers, film makers, etc. who address disappointments. Teens discuss whether triumph over tragedy is, or is not, part of the works they have cited.
b. Follow up with a *Creativity Festival* session in which teens explore different genres. Teens listen to music, view works of art, watch professional dancing, read prose and poetry aloud.

The Helper's High

Amusement parks, gifts, love, and vacations, have something in common,
a *high* or rush of pleasure.
Helping others activates the same pleasure centers of the brain,
resulting in *the helper's high.*

**The first step toward helping others is empathy; feeling another
person's emotions by "putting yourself in someone else's shoes."**

Empathy is about finding echoes of another person in yourself.

~ Mohsin Hamid

Example:
A teen basketball player feels empathy for children in poverty.
He starts a basketball free-throw marathon.
The sponsorship donations go to an organization that feeds and clothes kids.

What Echoes in Me?

I feel empathy for a person who is in this situation …

_____

_____

_____

_____

_____

I can put my empathy into action by …

_____

_____

_____

_____

_____

AFFIRMATIONS

Example:	My Own Affirmation …	My Action …
I have a heart that wants to help.		

The Helper's High

FOR THE FACILITATOR

I. Purpose
To acknowledge that helping others often results in a personal sense of well-being.
To put empathy into action.

II. Skills
Describe the *helper's high.*
Identify empathy toward people living with a specific situation.
State ways to help.
Take action to help.
Compose an affirmation with its accompanying action.

III. Possible Activities
a. Write on the board "Runner's High."
b. Elicit its meaning.
c. Teens share examples of natural highs they have experienced from exercise, an accomplishment, etc.
d. Distribute the *The Helper's High* handout.
e. Volunteers read the information, quotation, and directions aloud.
f. Teens complete the sentence starters, share their responses, and receive peer feedback.
g. A volunteer reads the affirmation aloud at the bottom left of the page.
h. Teens compose their own affirmation with its accompanying action; share aloud.
i. Teens cut out the affirmations and post them in prominent places (wallet, mirror, computer, *My Affirmations and More* display, etc.).

IV. Enrichment Activities
a. Teens with similar empathetic views of situations form teams.
   • Teams brainstorm and research ways to help and plan activities.
   • Teams share their plans and take action.
   • Teams report on their accomplishments.

b. The group forms one team and proceeds as noted above.

My Stream of Life

Think of your life as a stream.
Alongside the stream below, draw or describe one aspect of your life.
Use your imagination, or select one idea below:

My Favorite Memories
My Most Enlightening Mistakes
Fears I Faced
Times I Triumphed
People Who Helped Me Along the Way
My Future

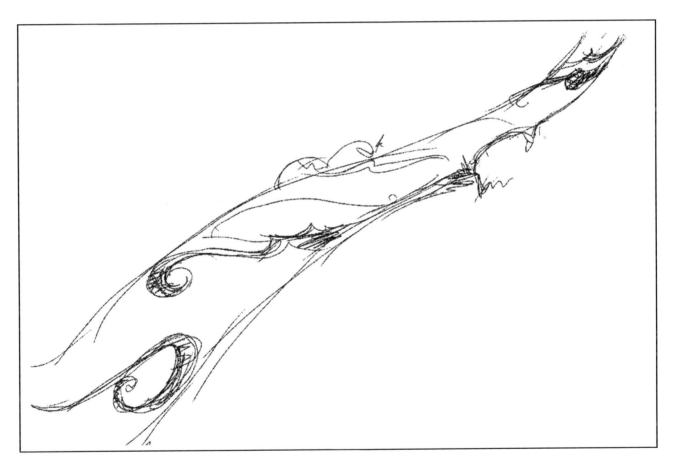

AFFIRMATIONS

Example:	My Own Affirmation …	My Action …
I remember the best and learn from the rest.		

FOR THE FACILITATOR

I. Purpose

To recall positive experiences and visualize future goals.

II. Skills

Describe the following and other teen-generated ideas:

Past positive memories

Lessons learned

Fears faced

Triumphs over obstacles

People who helped

Future goals

Compose an affirmation with its accompanying action.

Compose lyrics about obstacles that lead to positive outcomes.

III. Possible Activities

a. Distribute the *My Stream of Life* handout.

b. Volunteers read the information and directions aloud.

c. Teens complete their *streams of life*, share their responses, and receive peer feedback.

d. A volunteer reads the affirmation aloud at the bottom left of the page.

e. Teens compose their own affirmation with its accompanying action; share aloud.

f. Teens cut out the affirmations and post them in prominent places (wallet, mirror, computer, *My Affirmations and More* display, etc.).

g. Plan to use the same handout during future sessions.
   At each session, teens select a different idea to illustrate.

IV. Enrichment Activities

a. Write the following quotation on the board:
   "If it weren't for the rocks in its bed, the stream would have no song." ~ Carl Perkins

b. Teens interpret the meaning of *rocks* (obstacles).

c. Individuals or teams create song lyrics about the obstacles that lead to positive outcomes.

d. Teens share their lyrics and receive peer feedback.

My Soundtrack

**Like listening over and over again to the same favorite music and lyrics,
replay each day's positive events in your mind.
Remember and re-live positive moments as you drift off to sleep.**

Date	What happened today for which you are proud?	What happened today for which you are grateful?
Example: Sunday 6/11	*I gathered up some courage and talked to someone I've been wanting to get to know.*	*It's been raining all week and this morning the sun was shining and it shone all day!*
Sunday		
Monday		
Tuesday		
Wednesday		
Thursday		
Friday		
Saturday		

AFFIRMATIONS

Example:	My Own Affirmation ...	My Action ...
I focus on what went well.		

My Soundtrack
FOR THE FACILITATOR

I. Purpose
To remember positive actions and/or circumstances daily.

II. Skills
Record a positive action and/or a positive circumstance daily.
Compose an affirmation with its accompanying action.
Create a positive song title and lyrics.

III. Possible Activity
a. Distribute the *My Soundtrack* handout to each teen.
b. Volunteers read the information and examples aloud.
c. Teens recall the circumstances that happened yesterday.
d. Volunteers share their entries, and receive peer feedback.
e. Teens use the remainder of space for homework.
f. Volunteers bring their homework to a future session to share.
g. A volunteer reads the affirmation aloud at the bottom left of the page.
h. Teens compose their own affirmation with its accompanying action; share aloud.
i. Teens cut out the affirmations and post them in prominent places (wallet, mirror, computer, *My Affirmations and More* display, etc.).

IV. Enrichment Activities
Write on the board "My Upbeat Playlist."
- Teens brainstorm existing songs with positive lyrics.
- Individually or in teams, teens create new song titles with positive lyrics.

Kindness Kams

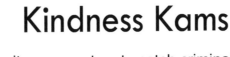

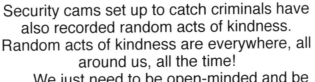

Security cams set up to catch criminals have also recorded random acts of kindness.
Random acts of kindness are everywhere, all around us, all the time!
We just need to be open-minded and be aware of these acts of kindness – and have the desire to do the same.

Take mental pictures of people being kind at home and in the community.
Each day, write or draw their actions on the left side of the Kindness Kam board below.
On the same day, write or draw your own random acts of kindness, at home and in the community, on the right side of the Kindness Kam board below.

Other's Random Acts of Kindness	My Random Acts of Kindness

AFFIRMATIONS

Example:	My Own Affirmation …	My Action …
I open my eyes and ears to kindness.		

Kindness Kams
FOR THE FACILITATOR

I. Purpose
To observe, remember, and perform, random acts of kindness.

II. Skills
Notice acts of kindness in one's life.
Recall mental pictures of kind actions observed at home and in the community.
Perform random acts of kindness at home and in the community.
Record the kind actions on paper.
Transfer the kind actions to a *Kindness Kam* Bulletin Board.
Compose an affirmation with its accompanying action.
View and discuss Internet videos of random acts of kindness.

III. Possible Activities
a. Before the session, provide large paper or a bulletin board for teens to write and draw on.
b. Distribute the *Kindness Kams* handout.
c. Volunteers read the information and directions aloud.
d. Teens record their current memories and random acts of kindness on the handout.
e. Teens transfer their descriptions onto the *Kindness Kam* Bulletin Board.
f. During subsequent sessions, invite teens to add their memories to the board.
g. A volunteer reads the affirmation aloud at the bottom left of the page.
h. Teens compose their own affirmation with its accompanying action; share aloud.
i. Teens cut out the affirmations and post them in prominent places (wallet, mirror, computer, *My Affirmations and More* display, etc.).

IV. Enrichment Activities
a. Teens research websites, view videos, and discuss the random acts of kindness.
b. Due to privacy considerations, teens are not instructed on the handout to take photos. Depending on school and community protocols, teens may wish to share photos of acts of kindness.

RECAP

Writing this record let me recapture who I am.
It is summed up in the title Be Not Nobody.
You need to feel comfortable in your own skin
and do whatever you need to do for yourself,
to heal or to grow.

~ Vanessa Carlton

Take-Away Skills

Conditions and Behavior (1), *Frequency and Duration* (2), and/or *Accomplishment* (3) statements for each activity may be used in educational and/or treatment planning, and also used to measure progress toward goals. These Take-Away skills promote real life outcomes and behavioral changes.

EXAMPLES

1. *Conditions and Behavior* – a skill or healthy habit to replace a previous less effective behavior or habit.
   - Now, I … *(less effective or undesired behavior)*.
   - When I … *(when do I do this?)*, instead I will … *(more effective or desired new behavior)* in _____ out of _____ opportunities.
2. **Frequency and Duration** – a skill or healthy habit not necessarily tied to a condition or previous behavior.
   - I will *(describe the behavior)* _____ times per _____.
3. **Accomplishment** – an outcome that is a one-time accomplishment.
   - I will *(describe the accomplishment)* by _____ *(date)*.

CHAPTER 8 - Recap
Take-Away Skills Examples

Accomplishment
   - *I will begin a new My Affirmations and More display, on the date that this one is filled up.*
Frequency and Duration
   - *I will document one positive action, every day for the next 6 months.*
Frequency and Duration
   - *I will send a hopeful message to someone, once weekly for the next 6 months*

128

Brush-Up BINGO

B 1-10	I 11-20	N 21-30	G 31-40	O 41-50
Why are affirmations recommended?	"My thoughts make or break me." Explain.	What is the value of having positive thoughts rather than negative thoughts?	Which of your positive traits is most important to you?	How can you be a positive role model?
Which situation in your life has contributed to your emotional growth?	Give an example of a time you were a Yay-Sayer.	Share a lesson you learned from your past.	"A failure does not predict my future." Explain	Share one of your strong beliefs.
What can you do when a negative thought pops into your head?	Give an example of re-programing a thought.	Share a positive and realistic thought about your future.	What can you do to make social media more positive?	Share a time when you turned CAN'T into CAN.
In what activity do you lose your sense of time?	What is your strongest motivator?	What does "Dance in the rain" mean to you?	How do you recharge your energy level?	How do you protect your mind from negative words?
What are you empowered to do in the next week?	What is outside of your personal control?	Share details about how you make a wise decision.	Is it easier for you to give or receive help? Explain.	Share a random act of kindness you witnessed.

Brush-Up BINGO

FOR THE FACILITATOR

I. Purpose
To review concepts about positive thoughts, affirmations, and actions.

II. Skills
Demonstrate personal application of twenty-five positivity concepts.

III. Possible Activities
a. Distribute the *Recap BINGO* handout.
b. Direct teens to number their pages differently from each other.
   Example:
   Under "B" one teen uses 2, 4, 6, 8, 10. Another uses 1, 2, 3, 4, 5. Another uses 1, 3, 5, 7, 9, etc.
c. The facilitator or a volunteer starts calling random letters and numbers.

B 1	B 2	B 3	B 4	B 5	B 6	B 7	B 8	B 9	B 10
I 11	I 12	I 13	I 14	I 15	I 16	I 17	I 18	I 19	I 20
N 21	N 22	N 23	N 24	N 25	N 26	N 27	N 28	N 29	N 30
G 31	G 32	G 33	G 34	G 35	G 36	G 37	G 38	G 39	G 40
O 41	O 42	O 43	O 44	O 45	O 46	O 47	O 48	O 49	O 50

d. Teens raise their hands and respond to the prompts when their letters and numbers are called.
e. Teens who prefer not to share may call on volunteers.
f. Teens mark the numbers they have responded to.
g. Teens win who have all numbers marked in vertical, horizontal, or diagonal rows.
h. Winners take turns calling letters and numbers.
i. Teens play until "Blackout BINGO" when everyone has marked all numbers.

IV. Enrichment Activities
a. Teens identify their most meaningful questions and responses.
b. Teens journal their responses.

POSITIVITY GAME SHOW

The Positivity Game Host writes these categories on the board:
**Affirmations – Traits/Qualities – Challenges – Re-programming Thoughts –
Enthusiasm – Self-Determination - Actions**
The game host reads aloud:
**"When it's your turn, choose a category. I will read the question.
You will respond, or you may ask others for help."**

Affirmations
Why are affirmations powerful?
Why do affirmations need accompanying actions?
Share your vision of you accomplishing a goal.
Why use the present tense rather than the future when composing affirmations?

Traits/Qualities
What is your trademark positive trait?
What trait do you want in your best friend?
What trait is most important in a partner?
Describe your favorite superhero's positive traits.

Challenges
What nourishes your emotional growth?
What can affect a person's emotional growth?
How can disappointments in your life be helpful later?
Share details about a time you overcame an obstacle.

Re-programming Thoughts
Give an example of a thought and its effects on feelings and actions.
How could changing your actions affect your thoughts and feelings?
How can people change their lives by changing their thoughts?
Share your ideas about a school's ideal social atmosphere.

Enthusiasm
What does real zeal mean to you?
When have you seen real zeal among students?
How do you motivate yourself to work toward a goal?
How do you keep your hopes up when you feel "down"?

Self-Determination
How do people change from helplessness to empowerment?
How can asking for help be a sign of strength?
Share a value that affects your decisions.
Share details about a time you kept an open mind and changed your decision.

Actions
Describe one of your most positive actions.
What does "Pay it forward" mean to you?
What creative activity helps you bounce back from a setback?
Create a motto about kindness.

POSITIVITY GAME SHOW
FOR THE FACILITATOR

I. Purpose
To review concepts about positive thoughts, affirmations, and actions.

II. Skills
Demonstrate knowledge by responding to twenty-eight questions.

III. Possible Activities
a. Explain that teens will play the Positivity Game Show.
b. Tell teens "There are no right or wrong answers. Respond based on what's true for you."
c. Distribute a copy of the *Positivity Game Show* handout to the volunteer host.
d. The host follows the instructions at the top of the handout.
e. Teens proceed according to the instructions.

IV. Enrichment Activities
a. Distribute the handout to all teens.
b. Teens journal personal responses to one or more questions in each category.